T0148057

# Codependency, *One Girl's Story*

*Lori Klauser*

iUniverse, Inc.
New York   Bloomington

# Codependency, One Girl's Story

*iUniverse books may be ordered through booksellers or by contacting:*

*iUniverse*
*1663 Liberty Drive*
*Bloomington, IN 47403*
*www.iuniverse.com*
*1-800-Authors (1-800-288-4677)*

*Because of the dynamic nature of the Internet, any Web addresses or links contained in this book may have changed since publication and may no longer be valid. The views expressed in this work are solely those of the author and do not necessarily reflect the views of the publisher, and the publisher hereby disclaims any responsibility for them.*

*ISBN: 978-1-4502-1689-0 (sc)*
*ISBN: 978-1-4502-1690-6 (ebook)*

*Printed in the United States of America*

*iUniverse rev. date: 03/23/2010*

# Chapter 1: My Past

Getting involved with a person who has a substance abuse problem is a common occurrence especially now days. It is estimated 10-20 million people are sick with the disease. Chemical dependency was formally recognized as a disease by the American Medical Association in 1956. Once a person becomes chemically dependent, he or she remains so forever. The 'disease' concept was hard to wrap my mind around. To me, it is a choice. So, choose not to drink I thought. Simple, right? Not so, says the medical community. Not being chemically dependent myself, it seems easy. If you don't pick up the drink or drug of choice, don't hang out with people who participate in that behavior, it won't happen. People who are chemically dependent, on the other hand, can't make the choice not to put themselves in that environment. 'Just one won't hurt', they reason.

Insurance company statistics indicate that within our society an alcoholic's life span is 12 years shorter on average. That is, if they continue to drink. The disease is treatable, though. Millions of people are recovering today. Of those that seek treatment, seven or eight out of every ten emerge successful. It is getting the person to admit to the dependency and then seek treatment that is the problem. I've heard it my whole life. "I don't have a problem." I heard it said by my dad to my mom; I heard it said to me by my ex-boyfriend, Brian.

I've also heard it blamed on others. Chemically dependent people place a lot of blame on others; it's just easier for them to deal with the outcome of their drinking. It is known as 'projection'. Dad would blame it on Mom and Brian blamed it on me. We heard that it was because of what we did that caused them to drink. I heard that it was my fault that Brian didn't come home at night. I was too much for him to deal with. He thought I nagged too much so he chose to stay out drinking all night. It's kind of like somebody saying 'the devil made me do it'. And, it is easier to do it again the next time if you can blame the behavior on somebody else.

Sometimes it comes down to the self-hatred the person feels within but will never admit to. It's about taking responsibility. Responsibility for your own actions and for the consequences those actions lead to. There are a lot of innocent people out there who take the blame that's placed upon them. Thinking if they had just said or done something different, this person in their lives would not be drinking or using the way they do.

It is believed by the person that has the dependency that it helps to relax, relieve stress or dissolve worries. And the nagging associated with the 'help' the other person is trying to give, leads to the drinking or drug use. It is rationalized by the chemically dependent person that the 'help' administered is nagging because they don't want to hear it. And, the chemically dependent person is usually the last to realize or admit that he or she has a problem. But for those of us involved in that person's life, it is the hardest thing to understand.

It is said that a lot of codependent relationships are weighed down with needs that went unmet as a child. Looking back through my list of ex's, most have had substance abuse problems. They say you always end up with a man just like your father. Outside of the drugs Brian used that couldn't be truer. You would think I wouldn't be one who got involved with a guy who has a substance abuse problem seeing that I grew up with a father who drank too much. It's hard to understand how a substance can take control of a person's thoughts, actions and feelings. Even though I had experiences in my life at a young age dealing with a problem that wasn't of my choosing, I didn't really understand the scope of the situation at that age, and I shouldn't have had to as a child. As an adult you have a choice, but making those choices can be hard when you love someone. Now I understand why my mom always stuck by my dad, no matter what. I learned from my mom's experiences that love doesn't give up, that love fights and tries hard to make things work. I did the same thing, for as long as I could until the threat of insanity was knocking on my door.

Growing up wasn't always easy. It's hard enough for the average person, but having to be caught in the middle of my father's alcoholic tendencies was rough. I never thought of him as an alcoholic, he just drank too much sometimes. I remember him always having a beer or two after he came home from work, but then there were those times when he went out drinking all night and came home drunk. I learned when I was young that being drunk wasn't a pretty sight. And I learned how to humor someone who drank too much to get them to eat something and go to bed. There are people who grow up to be alcoholics because that's what they grew up with and that's what they know. I was the opposite. I vowed never to drink like that, embarrass myself or hurt the ones I love in that way.

I remember growing up in the environment of a bar. I have memories of being in a bar since the time I was four or five (and the pictures to prove it). It never seemed odd to me, just what we did and where my family spent a lot of time. It wasn't until I was older that I realized that's not where most families spend their evenings. It never crossed my mind that there weren't any other kids around except my sister and me. We weren't in that kind of surroundings every night, mainly just the weekends. I do have fond memories of sitting at home watching television with my family (we liked the comedies) or playing games like Parcheesi. At the same time, there are also memories of my mom, sister and me walking to the mall some nights my dad didn't come home. We were only about three blocks away, so we were within walking distance. So, it was a partially normal childhood. The memories of dad's drinking are prevalent, though. The bad tends to take a front seat in your mind.

As a kid, I remember some horrific fights between my parents. Fights that involved a fire that started in our kitchen when Dad came home late one evening drunk. Mom threw dad's jacket on the stove and turned the burners on. The jacket was dropped on the kitchen floor and burned the tiles. The fire then proceeded to the backyard as the jacket was thrown out the backdoor. That was before we got our swimming pool in the late 70's.

There were also fights that involved glass breaking against walls and fights involving scissors that were used once to stab my dad's arm, along with a lot of yelling and screaming. I used to lie in bed when I was young, cover my ears and hum to myself to drown it out. I also recall my dad driving us home several times after the family had been in a bar all night and him clearly being impaired. This was before my mom learned how to drive. I would sit in the back seat with my head down, looking at my lap and praying that we would make it home safely. None of that is something a young child of seven or eight should have to deal with. When I was close to being a teenager, my mom started joining my dad at the bar. Maybe it was a "if you can't beat them then join them" sort of attitude. I just remember calling them almost hourly to see when they were coming home because I didn't want to be alone

I admit, I did have my 'drinking phase' I went through in high school. That's probably not abnormal now days. I was told by my sister that my mom was concerned about me. And who could blame her? She lived through my dad's drinking long before any of us kids were around. She was afraid I would follow in his footsteps. I didn't. High school was, well, high school. I did have my phase with Friday night parties. I always was the person who 'ran' the keg. I was extremely shy and that was a good way to meet people. I did drink a little in my early 20's, but then I didn't touch a drink until I was almost 30. I never drank to the point of getting drunk. It came down to a control issue. I did not want to lose control of my senses or who I was. I guess I was a social drinker. At the time, it helped me loosen up, but never to the point of not being in control. I was just out having fun with my friends.

I saw at a very young age everything that my mom went through and had to endure. She was understandably full of frustration and anger. But I also saw the strength that was within her. Later in life, I would understand what it is she went through. I would understand how it feels to wait up all night praying that your loved one makes it home safely. And I would understand how it feels to be consumed with the same kind of rage stemming from frustration and anger. I did not always feel strong, though people have told me that it took tremendous strength and courage to walk away from the life I lived and from the man I loved who not only was hurting himself but also me.

I vowed to never be in a situation like my mom was. My relationship with Brian has never been as bad as what I've seen as a child, but there were times it did get ugly. There was a lot of yelling and screaming, pounding on walls (a way of venting my anger), many nights spent worrying if he would make it home safe, praying to God he would and a lot of nights spent in separate beds. But before I went to the other bedroom, I made sure I told him what was on my mind and the way I felt. Silly me, I know the last thing you want to do is yell at a drunk. For one, did I think he'd even remember?

What they say is true, though, you can't choose who you fall in love with. As a child whose parents seemed to be in a codependent relationship of their own, there's a lot of powerlessness felt. There are a lot of things that are out of your control. To suddenly be in a relationship that mirrors what you grew up seeing is reliving the only thing you've ever know. I have had this outline of this book for over four years, but the hurt was still there and I couldn't proceed. I wasn't ready. I still had love for him. I still do today, just a different kind. I will always love Brian; I'm just not in love with him anymore. Following is my story; I'd like to share it with you.

# *Chapter 2: Meeting Brian*

I remember hearing that you marry a man just like your father. Granted, Brian and I never got married, but it progressed through the years to a situation that was close enough. After we had moved to Montana Brian frequently referred to me as his wife. I read an article once that explained the reason you marry a man just like your dad is due to the fact that there is unfinished business between you and your father regarding certain issues. Or, in other words, you attract yourself to a man like your dad because that's what you're used to and that's what is comfortable to you. Unfortunately, my relationship with Brian wasn't always comfortable. I always tried to humor my dad so he would just go to bed and leave us alone. You know how drunks always thing they're so funny? That was dad, but I just learned to humor him.

I never assumed I would love a man who had an alcohol and drug problem, but looking back, the track record I had was hard to ignore. I suppose I have a history of getting involved with addictive personalities. Many of my past boyfriends have had substance abuse qualities. Whether it was alcohol or drugs, the majority have been involved with one or the other or worse yet, both. Maybe I just always had the thought that I could save them. Only one has been involved with hard drugs such as cocaine and that relationship didn't last long. Within all these, there was a pattern there that I either did not see until it was too late meaning I had fallen in love with him or that I chose to ignore. I admit the latter might be true.

All of those relationships ended for one reason or another. Before I met Brian, I was building my life on my own, buying a car and a townhouse, but I wanted more. I wanted someone to share it with. After the record I had with men, it was scary. But I didn't want to give up. So, I moved on with a few dates here and there. Then I met a friend where I worked and we started hanging out together. She kept telling me that Brian and I should get together. After a year, she introduced us. I was 30 and Brian was only 22, which meant there was a total of eight and a half years that loomed in between us. Brian looked like a normal guy of 22. In the back of my mind, I knew he was young and wondered if he was ready for the serious dating scene. I didn't want someone who just wanted to have some fun. It was hard getting together in the beginning, missing phone calls and playing phone tag, but we finally did. The whole relationship wouldn't be easy as I came to see.

Brian wasn't exactly like my dad, in the sense that he progressed beyond just alcohol. I remember long before I met him, my friend had told me about the day she and Brian went to a mutual friend's wedding. She went on to tell about how they smoked pot together. My friend rarely smoked the stuff; in fact I don't remember a time she ever did besides then, so I assumed Brian didn't either. How wrong I was.

When you meet someone, it's almost like being in heaven. Nothing they do is wrong. It's like you see the world through rose-colored glasses. And you don't pay attention to the negative things people may say or the warning signs that arise. You don't want the perfect picture you've painted in your head to become tainted. And then there's the famous thought that he would change because he loves you so much. I'll touch more on that later.

It was a slow moving relationship in the beginning. He would only come over at night and we would talk and watch television together. Because he was very young, I think he was afraid to get involved with someone. And who can blame him; after all, he was very young. He spent many months being very distant. He did always keep in touch, even though weeks going on months would go by at times. We knew each other many months before we even went out together. Our first public outing was to Kmart. We went because I needed a computer desk. He even stayed for hours with me putting it together that night. By the time I knew that he had the same tendencies my dad had, though just in a different form, it was too late; I had already fallen for him.

My friend had warned me about the pot smoking. But, as I mentioned, I thought it was more a recreation thing. Little did I know he did it almost every day. Now, I'm no doctor, but I have done some research on the subject of marijuana. It has four times the amount of nicotine as a regular cigarette. And it is a well-known fact that nicotine is put in cigarettes to hook a person because of the addictive quality it carries. But someone who has the habit of either drinking or substance abuse doesn't want to hear the word addiction.

I didn't realize how frequent the pattern was until a few more months passed. Then one afternoon as we lay on the bed just talking, he told me he didn't want any secrets. I think the phrase he said to me was 'I smoke pot'. But hearing the words 'I smoke pot' didn't resonate with me. I knew he did, at least that one time, because my friend had told me about the wedding they attended together, but I still didn't realize that it was, in my eyes, almost a daily habit.

About a year after we had met, he moved in. It was more or less a fluke, I think. He had spent the night and after I left for work the next morning, he accidentally locked himself out of my townhouse. He locked then closed the door before he realized he had left the keys to his jeep inside. He had to use a screwdriver to pry his way back in as a neighbor looked on. He went over and explained what had happened; though I don't think she believed him. I never got a frantic message from my neighbor about what had happened with the key. It was after that, that I got a copy of my house keys and gently gave them to him. Logically, it made sense but since, in my eyes, he was a flight risk, I didn't want to scare him off. I didn't.

As our relationship grew, things surrounding the drugs became clearer to me. It was probably not until after Brian moved in that I realized the full extent of his drug use. He would go over to his sister's house, where he used to live twice a week to visit her, see his friends and to smoke pot. I assumed that's what he was doing over there, but I never realized that was the sole reason he went. Then one day I found his pipe under my couch. The only reason I found it was because my cat saw it and was pawing at it. I wasn't happy that he had brought it into my home and may have been doing it there too. There were only small glimpses into his drinking at that point that I occasionally saw. The coming home drunk rarely happened back then.

It did bother me that he did drugs, but I learned to put up with it. As long as he didn't do it around me, I was able to ignore it. Then there was the trip we took to Payson in northern Arizona. I had received a free stay in a hotel for inquiring about real estate. Brian and I decided to spend the day together there then take our free hotel room offer. We did have a wonderful time together.

We did drink whisky and cola on that trip, but he didn't drink to the extent I've seen him and his friends drink to later in our relationship. During the day when he was in the store buying a soda, I stayed in the car. I happened to open the storage compartment between the seats and found his pipe and a stash of marijuana. My thoughts went to the time Brian found $50 in that compartment that my dad had left for him because he worked on their air conditioner. I hoped my dad hadn't seen his 'stash'.

I was disappointed that he would bring that on a day's trip with me up north. Maybe it was just the place he kept it so maybe it wasn't like he purposefully took it along on our trip. I did wonder if he somehow took it with him when he went off into the woods to use the bathroom. So, I didn't say anything. It was the first of many times that I didn't say anything.

We also went on a weekend trip over one Memorial Day weekend to a camping ground outside of Young, Arizona. It took a lot of four-wheeling to get to the beautiful place we found. We could tell by the campfires that were apparent that others had been here before. After the first day, other campers showed up. It was such a beautiful place. In the early morning, deer would come and greet us as we started the campfire to keep warm. During the day it got hot out there, but the nights were very cold. Sleeping in the back of his Jeep wasn't the most comfortable, but it was an experience for me.

We had brought some Jack Daniels and soda and we played card games and drank. I did join him, and sometimes we would even drink at home. But at either of those times, Brian didn't drink to the point that I have seen him get to later in our relationship. He only drank a little that weekend. I guess I never would have noticed if he slid his pipe in the pocket of his shorts or not. After we were home I often wondered if when he went out to the woods by himself to use the 'facilities' if he had brought his pipe with him. One thing about Brian was that if he drank, he liked to smoke, if he started with smoking, he liked to drink. After time, I learned that one always led to the other.

There were good times we had. Good times where excessive drinking and/or drugs didn't get in the way. There were times when it was close to the picture perfect fantasy I had of our relationship. One thing I learned though is that you can't force things to turn out how they appear to be in your head. People make their own choices about their lives. Sometime those choices don't mesh with someone else's. No matter how hard you try; there's no escaping reality, no matter how long you try to postpone the inevitable.

# Chapter 3: The Move to Montana

Over time, I met his friends. My sister always liked the saying, 'birds of a feather flock together'. I never realized the extent of that until I met Brian and his friends. There are reasons certain people become friends - common interests. That's why I never hung out with people that did drugs. I don't do things like that, so why would I hang out with someone who does? Brian did though. There was that common interest.

And I learned that his friends did worse drugs than just smoke pot. They did the 'harder' drugs. Brian once told me he had tried cocaine, but he didn't like it. I even got to see the pictures of his spring break trip one year where they photographed the lines they had laid out of the drug in his jeep. I always told him if he ever started doing that to tell me because I would have to leave. I wonder if I would have, though. I should have left after I realized his smoking pot was an almost every day occurrence. You rethink things when you truly love someone. And you rationalize your moves and your decision not to leave.

There were actually a few times we hung out with his friends and his sister. It always seemed to revolve around drugs. There was even a time that we went with his sister and one of his friends to a movie. Of course, before we went to the movie they had to smoke some pot in the parking lot of the movie theater. It made me very uncomfortable and reminded me why I never hung out with his friends.

Then we went to Montana on vacation to visit his father and his family up there. We went with his sister and her boyfriend who happened to be Brian's friend. It was the most awful trip I'd ever taken. We drove separate cars and I kept hoping we'd lose them somewhere along the line, but we never did. There was one time along the way that we had to pull over so they could have a smoke. I stayed in the truck because I did not want to be among them and their 'habit'. Our luggage was in the back of the truck and I recall wanting to grab it out and hitchhike so I could try to find a way out of that nightmare. A little harsh, maybe, but if you don't join in to that activity, you feel so very much out of place.

When we pulled up to the motel the first night, once again, I thought we had lost them. Brian went back outside and soon after he came back in, I realized that we had not lost them at all and they were right there. I recall he had told me, if you could see the look on your face. I'm sure it wasn't pretty; I was angry. Many years later I would learn that his other half-sister wasn't much different. The same thing would happen when they went to visit her. At least that time, I was smart enough to stay home and go to bed early. The next morning I wanted to leave early thinking we could ditch them, but he made sure we waited and left together.

On that vacation, we also went to visit his grandmother, aunt and various relatives. I remember we went to see a movie, but Brian did not join us. It was some cartoon movie I can't remember the name of. It was good, but I was so focused on Brian and worried about what he was doing that it was hard to enjoy the movie as much as I should have. Again, I was worried about where he was and what he was doing.

Things moved along in the relationship as they normally would. Then came the day we spoke of moving. It's almost a blur to me how it came about. We had actually broken up not long before. Brian was the type where it took a while before he missed me and then doubted his decision to move out. At first, I had a hard time with the break-up, but by the time he missed me, I was feeling better.

So, we talked about moving. I had a choice. We could move to Cedar City, Utah; Reno, Nevada; or Ronan, Montana; Cedar City because that is where we stopped when we visited his family in Montana; Reno because he had passed through it while on vacation with one of his friends and his sister; or Ronan because that is where his dad and two half-sisters lived. I didn't want to live near casinos like the ones in Reno (even though there are several smaller ones in Montana) and at the time I didn't want to live in Utah, though Cedar City was an awfully cute little town. So that left Ronan. How bad could it be, I thought? His family is there and I heard it was beautiful. It had clean air; and it also had less traffic and crime than the big city in which we lived.

Being very close to my family, I didn't really realize the impact it would have on me. Brian was never very close to his family the way I am to mine. But I wanted to move with the man I loved; with the man I wanted to begin to build a future with. That's the way life is supposed to be, right? You move with the person you are in love with, and you begin your own family. That's what my mom did with my dad.

I do admit, I thought being away from his friends would change him. Lily, a friend of mine who has been a lifesaver in this situation laughed when I told her we were moving and calmly asked, 'You do realize everything will be the same, don't you?' But, I didn't. I saw us being 1200 miles away from the influence of his friends. I saw us being a happy little couple who could finally enjoy time together without them getting in the way. I saw a perfect life.

When you hear the words 'he won't change' it cuts like a knife. Of course he will, you think; silly them for saying that. They don't realize the influence I can have on him. I knew that with his friends nowhere near him, we will have that perfect life I dreamed of. He wouldn't even miss those kinds of friends and soon he would think back and wonder why he wasted time with those kinds of activities; silly me for thinking that. I didn't realize the influence those kinds of friends have on him. And a little secret – even if you move away, they make new friends just like the ones they leave behind.

I've often wondered how people with a chemical dependency find each other. Well, first they usually hang out in the bar scene. But how do people who do drugs find each other? It's something I may never understand since I don't inhabit that world. But apparently people talk after they've had a few beers and are in a bar. Because Brian found new friends just like the ones he had - some maybe even worse. And the old friends – well, they don't go away. Now they just happened to live 1200 miles away, but they would come to visit for at least a week at a time. And having them in your home is much worse than having your boyfriend go visit them in theirs.

Now don't get me wrong, they were nice enough guys. But I have a problem with people whose world revolves around either drinking or drugs. They would argue and say their lives don't revolve around the party life. I, of course, disagree. It seems to me like they can't enjoy themselves or have fun without drinking or doing some sort of drug first.

I found out that a small town in Montana would just fuel the fire. There wasn't much to do in a small town. Most things shut down by 6:00 p.m. After that, everything revolves around the nightlife, meaning bars. Now, I don't have a problem with bars in general. I don't have a problem with drinking. It's the fact that some people can't handle it and that's a problem for me. And Brian couldn't handle it a lot of the time. Maybe that's just my perception of it. I'm sure he would see it differently.

I was what you call a social drinker. Brian and his friends were drinkers who drank (as I saw it) with the sole purpose of getting drunk. I could sit at a bar for an hour with one drink. The bartender would continuously come over and ask if there was anything wrong with it assuming that I didn't like it. I guess they were used to people slamming them down, one after the other. If everyone drank like me, they wouldn't make much money.

In the beginning, Brian was home a lot. As time went by, he made more friends. He met people at his job and on job assignments. He started going to the bars more. Don't get me wrong; it's not like he would just leave me home alone. We would go together, but I didn't like to stay for hours upon hours. I was happy just having a few drinks then going home.

There's camaraderie when it comes to drinking. Brian had it with his friends back in Arizona and he was forming it with the new friends he was making. There's also camaraderie when it comes to the drug world. That's a world I didn't fit into. I can hang out in a bar for a short time, but I never could hang out around people who did drugs. There are people that can, who think its okay and they don't mind sitting there while people do the drug or pass a joint around, but it's just not okay to me. It's not okay to do it and it's not okay to sit in the same room and watch it being done.

That's one reason why Brian and I didn't do a lot together. I never went with him to visit his sister and her husband and kids. I didn't want to risk that being done. It was done a lot by them and I didn't want to be there when the kids weren't and they could sneak in a hit or two.

There were trips to the river I wouldn't attend because of the drinking and I assumed drug use that went on; those trips were near the end of our relationship. Even when we were on vacation before we moved to Montana, I remember a trip to the river with his family. Brian brought along a few joints. I remember because we got dumped into the river by the canoe we were in. He got mad because they had been in his pocket. I found that out when he laid out the joints he had brought in the sun trying to dry them.

When his friends were in town, it's like I was invisible. I wouldn't dream of tagging along there, but when his sister was in town there was a few times I would. There were times we went to lunch or walked around a summer festival. But the nighttime, that was theirs to do with as they wished. At first it was nice. I'm not very sociable sometimes and am an introvert, so I didn't mind the alone time. In the back of my mind, though, I longed to be a real couple that spent real time together.

# Chapter 4: Things Getting Bad

Life went on as usual. Day in and day out, there were bills to pay, dinners to make, clothes to wash and houses to clean. But the party times that Brian let his life encompass became more frequent. Maybe it was the way I reacted to it, but day-by-day it escalated and got worse.

Things didn't go bad right away. I put up with the late nights. It was okay to me as long as I didn't have to accompany him on his outings. There were times I would go to the bar with him, but like I said, I was okay with being there for a few hours and then going home. It was okay with me to go enjoy yourself and your friends, but not to stay out all night until the bar closed. Brian seemed to have to close the place.

A lot of it, I later learned, was because he wanted a girlfriend to accompany him on his ventures. He didn't want to appear as a single guy out there carousing around. And he wasn't carousing; he was just partying with friends. I used to joke with him that I never had to worry about him with other girls because the way he acted, not to mention the way he looked (his appearance) would keep them away from him.

Maybe he took slack from his buddies back in Arizona. He told me once after we first started going out that they would ask him, "Her? Are you sure?" Of course they didn't like me; I was nothing like them. I didn't drink like they did or do drugs. I think I was a threat to their way of life; the way of life that included their friend, Brian. They were afraid he would stop partying so much and they would lose him.

He is a nice looking guy, though. My neighbor mentioned that to me one day; about how good looking he was. But I still didn't worry about that sort of thing. I trusted him. One morning he told me that the previous night he was in a bar most of the night and that he had danced with a couple girls. They dragged him to the dance floor even though he protested. I know Brian hated to dance, but he let them drag him to the dance floor. For some reason, I wasn't that worried about it.

Like all addictions, it got worse. He came home late one night and walked up to the couch I was sleeping on. "I won," he said triumphantly. Puzzled, I asked him what he was talking about. When he was in a local bar, a girl started yelling at him saying that he didn't belong there. It was occupied by mostly Native Americans, and Brian did not fit the bill according to her. So she urged her boyfriend to beat him up. He said two guys followed him into the parking lot and one tried to jump him while the other stood back, obviously not wanting to get involved. Apparently, Brian got the upper hand and turned the tables. His fist looked like he had beaten the pavement. "I think he must have had braces," Brian remarked. I told him to go to bed. It made me ill to think about what had happened.

There was another night he came home, turned out the lights and began peering out the window. "They're after me," he said. Fearing it was another fight that happened, I made sure the door was locked. He went on to tell me that he had ditched the cops and he thinks they were after him. No one ever showed up at our door inquiring about him, so I figured it was a case of a wild imagination from drinking.

He even began hanging out with teenagers. His cousin was 17 at the time. He and his buddies would show up at the house a lot. They frequented the garage where they could 'smoke'. They were misguided kids who Brian was not helping to guide down a straight path. He thought he was though. They also helped him with his work, which was helpful to him, but my feeling is they did it because they knew they got to drink and also got free drugs, not to mention the cash he gave them for helping out.

I never slept much when he went out at night. I guess then I was the one with the wild imagination. But mostly I just worried about him getting hurt or even killed in a car accident if he chose to drink and drive. One evening he left at 8:30 and promised he would be home by 10:00. Hour after hour went by. He finally made it home at 4:00 in the morning. He wasn't as bad off as I've seen him in the past. He told me he had to save them, meaning his cousins and their friends. They were looking for trouble and he tried to steer them right. I supposed they would have gotten into worse trouble if he hadn't been there. And I know he had good intentions, but feeding them with alcohol and drugs wasn't helping either.

Another night soon after that, he went out and ended up calling me at 10:00 p.m. He told me he had crashed his truck and I had to come pick him up before the cops showed up. He tried to explain to me where he was, though I wasn't completely sure. He was about 30 minutes away on the way to Kalispell. He told me I had to turn onto one of the mile markers and I had a hard time finding it. I think I would have had a hard time even in the light of day, but I did what he asked, just like I always did.

The lake was to the left of me when I first driving there to find him. I remember driving past the end of the lake and I knew I had passed wherever he was. So I had to turn around. On the way back there were two raccoons that ran out in front of me. I was afraid to slam on the brakes because the lake was still right next to me down a small ravine, this time on the right. I remember one of them hitting one of the tires. I still feel guilty knowing I hit them or at least one of them. I had nightmares about taking one of them away from the other. I love animals and I would never do anything to hurt them. So instead of feeling the guilt, I blamed it on Brian. If he hadn't been drinking and driving he wouldn't have crashed his truck and I wouldn't have had to go out and try to find him at 10:00 at night.

I called him on my cell phone so he could try to explain to me where he was at. His cousin and friends were still with him so one of them came down to the road to let me know where they were. I think I finally found Brian about 11:00 p.m. He knew I wasn't happy with his actions. I knew he was very appreciative though, but it was just another time I had to go out of my way to save him from the trouble he, once again, had gotten himself into.

That was the night he had lost his wallet, so we went back to where they had been to see if we could find it. I didn't think much of it on the way up the road to where he had crashed his truck. We didn't find his wallet, but as we headed down the mountain I began to feel ill. On the way up we were on the side of the road that was against the mountain. On the way back down we were on the side of the road away from the mountain. There were a lot of switchbacks as the road curved around. The thought of him driving his truck on this road when he was drunk made me feel sick. There were not even any guard-rails, there was just a sudden drop off to the valley below; a very sharp straight down drop. I thought about how I wouldn't even know where he was or where to look to find his body! He always told me "I'm a good drunk driver", and I would always reply, "No, you're a lucky drunk driver and one day your luck's going to run out."

They always say someone on the outside can see so much more than what you can (or are willing to admit) to see from the inside. I've done it myself. You see women making all sorts of excuses for a guy who treats them badly and you wish they would open their eyes and see what you see. I think that was true for me for a long time. Then one day you realize that you have become that woman. I was helping to guide him I would say. If he didn't have me, he would be lost. Funny thing is you can't guide someone who doesn't want to be guided. They will turn and take the crooked path just to spite you. And worst of all, they will just drag you down with them.

I often think about all the energy that I used while I was in Montana. I was either trying to make Brian change or trying to allow myself to accept the things he did. For one, everyone knows you can't change someone to mold into the shape you find acceptable, even me. But, that didn't mean that I wouldn't try. I kept thinking maybe, just maybe he'll listen to me this time; maybe this time, something will sink in. That time never came though.

I tried to be more accepting of his ways. In the same way that I couldn't make him change from the things he did, I wasn't very successful at trying to make myself change either. Drugs were just not acceptable to me. No matter what, I knew I would never think it was okay. My sister always says that it wasn't any different than drinking. Okay, maybe, but drugs still are illegal no matter how you look at them and the situation.

I understand the concept she was trying to get to. Even I liked Brian better when he smoked marijuana than when he drank a lot and got drunk. He was much mellower. He could be a mean drunk unless you were sitting right there drinking with him. But I am so anti-drug that I would never think that it was okay to do any sort of drug; especially not illegal ones.

For that reason, we didn't spend much time together. Of course there were the times he took me out to dinner, the movies or we even spent time together riding his ATV. I enjoyed the times we spent hours just playing out in the woods. He always wanted to buy me my own, but riding together on his ATV was fun to me. To me, that was quality time we spent together. Those times were rare so I enjoyed every minute of them.

# Chapter 5: From Bad to Worse

I am amazed at how he made it through so many drunken nights. How he made it home safe without hurting anybody. There were many sleepless nights I had. I could never even fall asleep knowing he was out there and wondering what kind of trouble he was getting into. I thank God he made it home safely every night.

One thing addicts never do is admit guilt. Maybe that's because they honestly don't see anything wrong in the way they are acting. Or maybe it's because they won't admit to it. Like a child, they do not want to be scolded or told they are doing something wrong. I can understand that. And if that something is a thing that in the back of your mind you do know and do understand it is wrong, it gets even harder.

One thing I could never understand is how you can continue to abuse your body when the signs are right in front of you. It wasn't a usual occurrence but there were several times that Brian could not recall what had happened the night before. He would gaze into space, tell me to be quiet and say he was trying to piece things together, just give him some time and it'll come to him. Personally, I couldn't deal with not knowing what I had done the night before. That is a scary concept to me. The fact that he would admit this to me is amazing; especially knowing my feelings toward alcohol and drugs. But he tended to minimize the occurrences and adapt to them.

The nights got longer, too. In Montana, the bars stayed open till 2:00 a.m. instead of the 1:00 a.m. we were used to in Arizona (though that has now changed). There were times he would stay out until 3:00, 4:00 or even 5:00 a.m. at 'after parties' as he called them. After the bar closed, they would move the party to someone's house so they could keep drinking or using.

There were also the times he would purposely stay out till 5:00 a.m. to 'teach me a lesson'. He knew it would get to me, so he purposely parked somewhere and slept it off. These nights weren't spent partying; they were spent sleeping in his truck in an empty lot somewhere. I wonder if he just passed out somewhere. He admitted that to me one day. It helped ease the thoughts that went through my head some evenings as the hours dragged on.

I didn't get a whole lot of sleep the nights he stayed out late. I was so worried about something bad happening to him. I worried about the accidents that could happen, that the cops out there trying to keep everyone safe who could pull him over and haul him off to jail. That was a better thought than the others. Hearing sirens throughout the night was pure torture to me. My imagination played out the worst scenarios in my head, especially after seeing the drop off on that mountain side.

I think there may have been one night that he did go to jail. I vaguely remember him mentioning while on the phone to one of his friends that he had called his half-sister who also lived in our town and she picked him up. I'm not sure what night that was though. I remember calling in to work a few times because I was so tired that I couldn't function. Either that or I would go for a short time then go home.

Then there were the few times he drank so much he threw up. It was usually when he didn't eat dinner. The first time he blamed that on me too. He went out drinking in the afternoon and got buzzed. He was afraid to come home to eat lunch because he knew I would lay into him about his drinking. Honestly, I probably would have, but it would have been better if he had come home to eat. And I just didn't understand.

There is food in every bar I've ever been in. We used to eat at some of the bars we went to; sometimes lunch, sometimes dinner.

By the time he did make it home at 5:00 p.m. he stood on our deck, leaning over it to throw up in the back yard. I sat there in the patio chair watching. I think that upset him more. I just wanted to know why. He wasn't very talkative at the time. And I knew better that to try to talk to a drunk or intoxicated person, but I did it anyway most of the time. I had so much anger bottled up inside it became hard to pretend it didn't bother me. I just wanted answers as to why?

He came inside later to lie down for a while. I offered to make him dinner, which he agreed to. Afterwards, he asked me why. Why would I make dinner for him? I explained that I loved him and that's what women like me do. I want to take care of him. I was also afraid he'd go out and drink some more and I wanted to keep him home.

The next time he went out drinking and came home late, which was around 1:00 or 2:00 a.m. was the next week. I remember hearing his truck pull in the driveway, but he never came inside. After several minutes, I looked out the bedroom window. I saw him leaning over the deck again. After several more minutes, I looked out again. He was sitting in one of the patio chairs. It wasn't for another 10 minutes or so till he finally came in.

Then there were the times his friends from Arizona or Vermont came to visit. I dreaded those times. They were nice enough guys, but the drinking usually ended up out of control. I saw them one night in the garage downing whiskey. After that they went out to the bars. I guess they had to get 'buzzed' first to be able to enjoy themselves. One night after they came home, one of his friends apologized to me. He said he was sorry. That was nice but not enough.

I started keeping track on my calendar of the nights he went out, the time he came home, and the nights he was drunk or not. I started doing that in the beginning of 2004. I also started getting migraines around that time. So, I highlighted the party nights in yellow, the migraines in pink. Funny how those two things never seemed to tie in together for me. It was a 'duh' moment for me when I realized the connection.

We also used to have a bigger calendar that Brian used to keep track of his work jobs and what was scheduled and when. He had written 'sick' on a day when he didn't work because he was hung over. Later that night, I wrote 'liar – hung over!' I wasn't sure he would find the humor in that, but he did. I guess it's good that you can laugh at yourself.

None of the circumstances deterred him from not continuing the drinking; not the memory loss, not the throwing up over the deck, not the missing work because of it. And most of all, my lectures I gave because I was impelled to and thought I was steering him in the right direction didn't. It was a hard lesson for me too. One that was hard to comprehend. How someone cannot see (or admit to) the destruction they are causing in their own lives and in the lives of the ones that love them was a mystery to me. It is a frustrating thing. You want to shake the person and yell at them. That, of course, isn't going to help; nor did the lecturing that I did. I didn't know what else to do. I had so much frustration and anger bottled up inside of me; I'm surprised I didn't explode more often. I thought one of those times something would sink in and he would understand.

A friend told me recently that Brian probably didn't even like himself very much. But to admit that to another, especially a close loved one would be unbearable and embarrassing. Guys in general like to appear and look strong to the outside world and especially to their friends.

The drinking probably was an ally to him. It probably helped him to feel better. He didn't see himself as out of control. He didn't see himself as someone who needed help. He probably liked himself better when he drank. It probably helped him feel on top of the world. I'm sure it was a way of helping him to handle what I saw as a problem.

I say probably because I do not know what he was or is feeling inside. The two things I know for sure about Brian is that he does not want to grow old and he does not want to be alone. That's probably why he wanted me to be with him when he went out partying. I'm sure the drinking and drug use made him feel young, probably made him feel that he could hold on to that feeling and never grow old. And he wanted to share that with me.

I was very different than that though. I had my moments when I was younger, but I also realized there's a time when you have to grow up. There has to be a time when responsibility is important. Imagine if the whole world was just interested in having a good time. I guess I came to learn that there are much more important things.

I was interested in having a family of my own one day too. I guess I always knew that if we did that that would be a hard thing. We had such different views of things how could we raise a child? I always knew that I'd be preaching that drugs were bad and wrong. And Brian would be out in the garage rolling a joint with him or her.

I had a friend a long time ago that had a sister whose husband did drugs. They had a son and when he became a teenager his mom tried to tell him that drugs were wrong. His question to her was, what about Dad? He knew his father did them but his mother didn't and she told him how wrong they were. I didn't want to end up in a situation like that.

# Chapter 6: Trying to Stay Sane

Within the grips of an addiction, the one not addicted tries to hang on to some sense of normalcy. They try to keep up with life as normally as they can. They try to hang on to the life they once knew – life before the addiction started. And most of all, they want to keep up appearances to the outside world. Why let anyone else know the secrets of the life they hide? The logic is that no one could help anyway. Logic tells you that they wouldn't be able to get through to him and they wouldn't be able to comfort me.

Seeing as we were not together the majority of the time Brian went drinking, it probably appeared as it was to most. I didn't think his drinking friends whether they were in Montana partying with him or the ones back in Arizona ever gave a second thought to me. Everyone knew that I never shut down a bar in Montana and I never went with him to visit any of his friends or relatives who did drugs; I kept myself separate from that world. I was different and I knew I wouldn't fit in.

There were several times I missed work because he was out all night. I couldn't sleep when I didn't know where he was. I would try, but it never worked if I didn't know where he was or what he was doing. My imagination always got the best of me and made up stories; stories that never had a happy ending. I knew my imagination took the worst scenario possible and embellished on it. I knew that, but I still let it affect me.

There were times I went to work, putting forth my best effort, but left shortly after because it's hard to function on a job when you get little to no sleep. Brian was self-employed so if he didn't feel like getting up and working, he didn't have to. He did have a job working for someone else when we lived in Arizona and somehow he never seemed to have a problem. Maybe because owning your own business makes you have to do things on other people's schedules; there wasn't a set time every day that he had to be somewhere to do something unless he had an appointment. He had control of his work life even if he didn't seem to have control over his personal life.

On top of working full time, I was trying to start a writing career. It was hard to focus on when your world is going out of focus. I think I got to the point where I didn't care about myself or my dreams. My main focal point was on him. I tended to concentrate more on Brian than on myself. I wanted to take care of him. I wanted to nurture him. I wanted to make him better. I was just going about it the wrong way. I wasn't helping, I was harming. He was defiant and because of my actions, his reactions were detrimental to himself. And without realizing it, they were detrimental to our relationship and to me too.

My anger started getting the best of me too. There's only so long you can keep it bottled up within yourself. We had a hard time talking anything out because as he saw it, I would lecture and as I saw it, he just would rebel. Neither one of us listened very well either. Then it got to the point of yelling. It seemed we both wanted our own way. I saw it as trying to fix our relationship, he saw it as me trying to change him and control him.

I became so angry I would yell at him, leave the room and pound on the walls. I was so frustrated with the situation; I didn't know what else to do. Pounding on the walls was the way I took out my anger. I couldn't imagine any other way to handle it. And the more he rebelled and didn't listen, the angrier I became. This was very out of character for me. I do not like confrontation, nor do I like to fight. By pounding on walls I wasn't hurting him or anyone else, just myself.

As the anger built, it got so bad that one day I resorted to picking up a framed picture on the television and throwing it at him. I had no intention of harming him; after all, I threw the frame at his feet. I didn't like what I was becoming though. And the bad times and the anger I had were coinciding with my headaches. They got more frequent and more severe, to the point that I would spend all day in bed, my right eye watering. I guess it looked like I was crying, though only out of one eye!

On top of yelling, screaming and throwing things, I began biting my nails; a nervous habit I guess. I always had pretty long nails, but suddenly I had begun biting them. I chewed on them until they would rip at the corners. Suddenly, they were just little nothing nails, just nubs. I tried putting nail polish on them thinking if they had pretty colors on them then I wouldn't touch them and they could grow back. Wrong. I bit them all the same.

Even Brian mentioned to me once, 'What happened to your nails? You always had such long pretty nails.' Hmm, I wondered. I wanted to yell at him what do you think happened to them? You happened to them. I wanted to tell him to look in the mirror and there he would find his answer. It seemed to be due to my worrying about the situation. I worried about what would happen to our relationship; I worried about what would happen to him if he continued this kind of life. I was last on my list. I hardly ever worried about myself. My focus was on him.

Then there was the day I went outside to water the flower beds. It was at the exact moment that a police car was driving by our house that I noticed a marijuana plant growing among the flowers. I prayed that they didn't notice. That's all I needed was to be dragged down with him because of his bad habits. I started thinking about the ways his life would impact mine. It may have been all fun and games to him, but I started being concerned about my own welfare.

I would talk to my mom every Sunday. She would ask how things were; just fine I would always tell her even if they weren't. How could I tell my mom (who was 1200 miles away) the kind of life I lived? She would just worry endlessly. Maybe that's where I get it from. They say that 90% of the things we worry about never happen. I would imagine in my head the worst case scenario. Why didn't I spend time imagining a happy scenario? Maybe I was just trying to be prepared for the worst case scenario just in case it happened.

The walks with our dog out in the field kept me happy. Sometimes my mind would wander to the happy life that I wanted and dreamt of. As I watched our dog go running, happy as can be, I envied him. Dogs hardly have a care in the world. He was so happy; as happy can be to go out in the open field and just run for as long as his energy held up.

No matter what I did, Brian was the focus of my attention. The times I went to the mall in Missoula with friends, I would be focused on him, wondering if he was home yet, wanting to hurry and get home. I couldn't even enjoy myself. He was always my main focus no matter where I was, what I was doing or who I was with.

I met a new friend not long before I left. We went to the mall in Missoula, which was an hour away from where we lived. The whole time my mind was focused on Brian. When we returned home later that afternoon, he was home having dinner. I did briefly stop to think of the fact that he goes on with his life making dinner for himself. I would never do that, I would always be worried about him, where he was and what he was doing. My friend and I had stopped at a garden shop and I bought rose plants for our front yard before we came home. I think I knew then that I wouldn't be there very much longer, yet I was always still only trying to please.

After I left I kept in touch with that friend for a short time, but in the back of my mind I worried about the two of them. Now that I had introduced them, maybe they had gotten together. That's part of the insanity that you lower yourself to. You're always thinking about the what if's. You imagine every scenario that you can and then you worry about what you created in your mind then I worried about it coming true.

Maybe all that really is is a part of me that is trying to protect myself; a part of me that wants to keep harm away from me. Maybe it's just trying to get me ready just in case the scenario presented itself. It just wanted to keep me alert. I also think it was a case of letting my imagination get away from me. Kind of like that night Brian thought the cops were following him and were after him. The only difference was that I wasn't drinking or doing drugs.

I know that along the line, I made mistakes. I made mistakes that harmed me and I made mistakes that harmed Brian. He was defiant and would rebel against what I thought was help, but he saw as trying to change him. I knew enough that if someone knew you were trying to change them, your chances of that happening are pretty slim. And no matter what I did, Brian seemed to be defiant in his ways and thoughts.

I don't blame him. I know it wasn't his fault. I can be just as stubborn. He didn't believe he was doing anything wrong. This was a way of life to him and his friends. Why should I expect him to suddenly jump on my band-wagon and believe the things I believed? I knew it wasn't that easy to get someone to believe my way of thinking. How could I expect him to change? Would he expect me to change in the same way? He knew I wouldn't, so why would I expect him to?

# Chapter 7: Wanting Me to Join Him

You assume that most people who drink hang out with others who drink. That was partially true for Brian. He had a lot of friends who drank and did drugs. Those are the people you know you can count on when it comes to partying and when you're looking for 'supplies' for your habit. That's probably why people didn't understand our relationship and why his friends didn't think we were right for each other.

Once after we had been dating for a short time, Brian told me that he was glad I didn't drink and do drugs. It was a nice place for him to fall, a safe haven. I'm sure that lifestyle can get crazy. I don't know, I don't inhabit that world. Soon after we had moved to Montana he told me that I keep him grounded. That it was nice to have a normal life to come home to.

Maybe that kept me thinking that eventually he would change. He would see my way of life as something he might like to aspire to. He would see the calmness of it. He might even come to like the serenity. I thought that seeing my way of life might influence him to change. It might help him to see that it is a better life than having to worry about the police following you and what the outcome could be of your drinking.

I guess it's just an acceptable way of life for people who do drugs. It's just part of that kind of life. It's not anything out of the ordinary. If you go to jail tonight, someone will be there to bail you out and you can go about your life tomorrow. It's not a big deal unless you become a repeat offender. But next time you will just figure a better way to go about illegal activity.

Even if he did see it that way, he knew he would have to go out on his own to drink. I have a hard time staying out as late as you have to shut down a bar. I like to enjoy myself but that enjoying doesn't include getting drunk or wasted, or being there as late as you need to be to shut down a bar. That's just not fun to me. I guess I just know when to stop. Brian felt differently though. He liked the feelings that he felt when getting 'buzzed', but he didn't know how to stop. He would continue until he was past the point of being buzzed and before long he would be on his way to being drunk.

I don't find the people within that environment amusing either. I recall several times that I was in the bar with him and many people who obviously had consumed way too much alcohol tried talking to me. Besides not being able to understand their words, it was hard to understand the concept they were trying to relay. I have no patience for anyone like that, nor did I understand the concept. There has to come a time that it is no longer fun because you are stumbling about unable to see, stand or walk. It just reinforces my way of thinking to me; that being past the point of just being buzzed was not an attractive way to be.

We went canoeing once with his family. That included uncles, cousins and sisters. That was the year we went on vacation with his sister and a friend of his whom she was dating at the time. I remember not having much interest in going canoeing. I would have rather have stayed home with his mom and grandma. I would have been more interested in watching TV or reading, but his mom insisted I go.

I learned later that Brian had brought a couple joints with him in his fanny pack when we went out canoeing. He was very upset when our canoe had toppled over so his fanny pack got wet. I didn't' realize what was in it until we stopped later and he laid the joints out on a rock to dry. This was one reason I didn't want to go canoeing. I never knew what to expect. And this is the reason I worried about going on vacation with him. Maybe it would have been better if we had been alone. I knew that being with some members of his family would result in situations like this. They didn't care how I felt about it, why would they?

Brian always said he wanted me to accompany him to such functions such as parties. I did once to a Christmas party at someone's house where there was a band. The band was good but having to watch my boyfriend stand around in a crowd of seven or so people as they passed a joint around the circle was not fun. It was something you'd expect to see a high-school crowd doing not adults. It has always bothered me that I got back in his truck with him and he drove us home. I think I was very lucky that we did not get in an accident or that we were not pulled over by police.

So, needless to say, Brian and I didn't do a lot together. I longed to have a boyfriend I could do things with, someone I had more in common with, someone I didn't have to be afraid to go out and do things with because I was afraid he'd start drinking too much or pull out drugs and start smoking them. Granted, we could go to the movies or out to dinner, it was hard finding anything else we could do as a couple. I was even afraid to go on a vacation with him, afraid that he would have to bring along his drugs. There was so much I wanted to do with him, so many places I wanted to go, but I was afraid to even go on a simple vacation with him.

A friend of mine told me about Mount Rushmore. She told me about the vacation she took with her husband. They went on the Fourth of July and there were fireworks above the presidential faces. I wanted so bad to go, but I was afraid to mention it to Brian; it's not that I was afraid he'd want to go – I think he would have – I was afraid that if we did he would find a way to bring drugs.

I was afraid to ask him on any vacation. We came down to Arizona together once. He dropped me off at my family's and he went to stay out with his sister. He actually had my car at the time, which bothers me now knowing he probably drove to a bar that night with my car. I still don't know. All that mattered at the time was he (and my car) made it back in one piece when we were supposed to drive home to Montana.

I guess I forfeited a lot of happy times worrying about him. I just didn't want the drugs to be part of my life. It was just something I was so against, it was hard to ignore. Maybe part of me was trying to be right. It took me a long time to come to the conclusion that we just lived life from different viewpoints and both of those had different rules. And even longer to realize that he wasn't going to change and if I was to live my life under the rules I saw as 'correct' that he probably couldn't be a part of that life.

I just couldn't stand to think of me being without him. Even though I didn't agree with his way of life; I couldn't imagine us not being together; of us not sharing a life. I struggled so much against it that was all that entered my mind. That's what I was focused on all the time. I tried to imagine ways that I could change him. Things that he would think were acceptable and show my love for him.

# Chapter 8: Times he Admitted He Had a Problem or Needed Help

There were times Brian actually admitted that he had a problem. Times he said he needed my help. Those were the times that he had a hard time functioning the next day due to a hangover. That was early on in our relationship and those times didn't last long. Later when the problems got worse, he seemed to not recall those times or that he said that. In time, he outright denied it. He even once told me – I don't have a problem. True, the problem was mine because he did not believe he had a problem; it was me who could not handle his drinking or drug use.

Everyone always told me to take care of myself. Even his own mother offered that advice a couple times to me. She just outright told me to leave. She had dealt with Brian's father and his drinking. She eventually walked away from that relationship. Within the time I was there, his aunt also walked away from her husband because of his drinking. His grandmother even told the man she was with to stop drinking or it was over. Because he did not stop soon after that, she ended the relationship.

It was beyond my comprehension that all the women in his life had spouses or partners who had a drinking problem and they actually walked away from these men yet Brian did not acknowledge that he had the same kind of problem. Don't you think something would trigger something in his mind that said maybe drinking as much as I do or doing drugs isn't a good thing? Maybe the relationship I have might end that way too because of the things I do.

To see so many relationships in his life ruined because of drinking, yet not change to even slightly cut back on drinking and to lessen the effects it had on his life. It was a world I did not understand. How can a drink or a drug give you more comfort than a real person in your life who wants to help you? I did not understand why he couldn't see that and allow himself to make things better?

I slowly began to see the word 'codependent' in my life. Not long after I left, I found a book on the subject that seemed to be calling out to me from the bookstore shelf. I was in the self-help section of the bookstore. I'm not sure what led me to that section, but it seemed subconsciously to know what I needed. I saw all the books on the subject and thought, 'Wow. I'm not the only one that this affects.' This was after the damage had been done. It was still hard for me to understand how or why Brian would not change.

So, I bought that book that was written by Melody Beatty titled "Codependent No More" and by the time I got to page 7 I found a whole description that could have had my name above it. It was me to a tee: the rage, the bitterness, the hatred, the fear, the depression, the helplessness, the despair, the guilt. I had felt all those at one time or another. I realized I was out of control. Maybe I hadn't helped the situation. Maybe it wasn't his entire fault. Granted, he still had a substance abuse problem, but maybe I hadn't helped the situation by the way I reacted. It is never just one person's fault. It is always a shared responsibility.

I met a dear friend of mine at a job I worked at years before I met Brian. It took years for me to learn that she too had an addictive personality as she puts it. She has lived through the horrors I was living through with Brian, though, Lily was on the other end. She helped me see a different viewpoint than my own. She helped me see things as Brian saw them because Lily also was an addict to the drugs.

It was an eye opening analysis of the other side of the coin. Aside from chocolate there was nothing I couldn't say no to, especially when it came to things like drinking or illegal substances. Maybe I was just too afraid to even try any of it, but I knew even long before I met Brian that things like that were bad news. And fortunately I never had the tendencies to take part in that sort of activity.

Lily still to this day goes to AA meetings. She says it's a hard thing to go through, that the substance is one you must struggle with every day. Going to the meetings helps though. It helps as you talk to people who have also been through the situations you have been through, situations that are an ongoing effort to deal with. It helps you feel like you're not alone. That's another reason why I should have gone to those AA meetings.

Lily has been there to listen to me as I cried about the difficulties I endure. She has helped explain to me the other side of the situation. Since she has been there herself, she has given me an in-depth look at an addict's point of view. She has relayed the feelings to me that she has felt, that she herself has struggled with. She explained to me the great energy she has to exert to deal with the feeling of addiction. She has explained the symptoms that pertain to an addict's lifestyle.

She also explained to me how it changes a person; not only the addict, but also the person who was trying to help the addicted. That was something I was slowly starting to see. If you are the person trying desperately to help another with a substance abuse problem, you don't even notice when it happens to you. The anger builds slowly that by the time you notice that you yourself have a problem it may be too late.

Lily always told me to go to Al-Anon meetings, but I never did. I wish I had. They did have them in Montana. They held them not far from where we lived. I never understood why they were held on Friday nights. Maybe they figured people who need to attend those meetings would be alone on that night; that their significant other would be somewhere other than at home on a Friday night. Maybe they assumed they'd be in a bar.

That is probably assuming too much. They also held them on Tuesday nights. I think I was so consumed with where Brian was on any given night, I was afraid to rock the boat. I was afraid of what he would think or say if I had gone to a meeting. I wasn't one to share the world I lived in with hardly anybody, let alone a complete stranger.

I also was afraid to be single again. I was afraid to have to go out there and meet people. I'm not the most social. In fact, I'm very anti-social. It takes a lot to feel comfortable around people; I am very shy. So to me it seemed acceptable to stay where I was. I have already proved that I can put up with the situation I was in. My friends would be my friends no matter if I lived in Montana or came back to Arizona.

Lily should know; she's the one that received the brunt of my codependent ways. She's the one that had to listen to the crying, the anger, the resentment, and the hurt that I stored up inside of me. She's the one that truly tried to help, but I'm sure felt very frustrated as the years went by as I stayed but continued to cry to her about the fate I chose to live in.

Lily once told me how a life like what I was leading changed people. It changes the core of who you are, she said. Where once a happy go-lucky girl lived within, a cold, afraid, timid, always on the lookout for someone whose intention it was to hurt her was lurking. I admit I was afraid to trust anymore. I was not sure if people were being honest with me or not. I didn't want to hurt like I had in the past.

It was my choosing because the thought of being alone was scary to me. After so many years, the thought of going back to being single was not attractive to me. I had a dream of finding a man I loved and building a life with him. I didn't want to let go of that. After so many years of being alone, I couldn't bear the thought of living life on my own again. I knew I could take care of myself; I mean I always did, but after finding someone you fear going back to the emptiness of living life on your own.

I admit I am very stubborn, but I did not want to cave and admit defeat. I knew I could make this relationship work. After all, all those years of our relationship I felt like it survived because of me. I thought I was the one that held everything together; I was the one that compromised most of the time. If I had survived for nine years, why couldn't I survive as I did for nine more years and then some?

Now, I wish I had attended those Al-Anon meetings. Maybe that would have salvaged things. In my mind, though, that was a big maybe. Sometimes you have to look at the bigger picture. Maybe someone much higher up had a different plan for my life and for his too. Maybe I was wrong and we weren't mean to be together. That was something that would take years for me to admit. Once you find what you think is going to be forever, you don't want to let go of it.

Many times Brian told me how he wasn't impressed with himself. He didn't like the way he was acting or the things he did. It was usually after one of his late nights out when he would come home drunk and have a hangover. The next day he would feel awful and say how he didn't impress even himself. But there were so many times I heard that, I thought one of them would finally sink in and change things. That never happened. I convinced myself that one day it would though.

I held on to what he had said. The words it won't be like this forever actually came out of his mouth early on in the relationship. It might have been near the time he told me he wasn't impressed with himself. I think he knew that his body wouldn't allow him to continue this kind of lifestyle. When you're young, you don't worry about the future. You don't worry about the fact that your body will not always allow you to live like this. They just want to enjoy the here and now; they'll think about the future when it shows up.

One thing I never seemed to take into consideration was my future. I was setting that aside, too. The only thing that mattered to me was Brian. In a roundabout way I did care about myself, I guess. But I always saw myself as an extension to him. If he was going to be healthy, I would be too. We were one in the same in my head.

I guess I figured if I could make him healthy, I would be too. What I didn't realize is that I had to work on myself first. Now I'm not saying always but sometimes when someone sees that you care about yourself then they will follow your direction. I tried in my own way to make Brian follow me. Unfortunately, I went about this the wrong way. You can never make anyone follow you or try to bribe them to follow your ways.

I think if it was meant to be, it would have been easier. I did not want to admit or even think about the fact that we were not meant to be together. That just wasn't acceptable to me. I believed that I could make him see the light and follow me in my way of life. How could it not be better than the life he was leading?

You always see what could have been if you had dealt with it in another way after the fact. But who's to say that the life I was trying to show him we could have would have lasted very long. If it wouldn't have truly been his decision, who's to say it would have lasted at all or that the hurt wouldn't have been even worse? Believing that someone has changed and seen your way of living as better than what he was living would have hurt worse when I realized that he wasn't going to truly give this way of life a try. It would have hurt worse to expect him to change and then realize that it wasn't going to be the way I saw it in my dreams.

# Chapter 9: Wasted Time

I watched unable to help. As I watched Brian, time ticked by as he wasted his time in a clouded state of mind. We had some good times in the beginning of our relationship. He wasn't always in a clouded state of mind. It might have been because I was oblivious to the fact that this was not only a social matter with Brian but also a way of life.

I think I was oblivious to the fact that this might just be his way of life. That it might last longer than I realized. I held on tight to the dream life I had in my mind; the perfect life with a picket fence around the house and children playing in the yard. No one could rip that dream away from me, I wouldn't allow it.

There's one thing we cannot do in this life is choose how another will live their life. It is always up to the person. He or she is the one that will have to answer for every decision they make. Even if they change because someone else wanted them to, that is a decision they will also have to answer for.

Looking back, I remember a time not long after we met when he told me he wanted no secrets between us. He let me look thru a box of old pictures he had and we talked about whom the pictures were of and the circumstances in which the picture was taken. I can't even remember all the circumstance or the people, but I do know that there were pictures of bongs and such that were drug related. I then took out a lot of old pictures I had and we did the same thing. My pictures weren't of people and parties they were just of friends hanging out at the pool or in their houses or backyard with no mention of drugs of any kind. Just another example of the different kinds of life we each led.

That helped somewhat in understanding where he was coming from, but to me, the thought of having to put some chemical into my brain to 'make' myself think I'm having a good time or that everything is okay is just plain sad in my point of view. Maybe we just have different ideas of what fun is or what it constitutes. To me fun isn't about losing control or doing or saying something you'll be embarrassed about later, or not even being able to remember the facts for that matter.

I couldn't understand why he couldn't just stop. Why he couldn't or wouldn't choose me and having a great relationship over the substance that I saw him abusing? He always told me he did choose me; that he loved me 'dearly'. The one thing he loved to remind me of is that he came home to me every night. Even though sometimes it might not be until 4:00 a.m., he still came home to me. My argument was that he owned our home too and that's why he came back because it was his home. He wasn't coming home to me, he'd go there even if I wasn't there, and after all, it was his home too.

Maybe I was making the whole thing too difficult. I was stubborn and I was upset that he didn't see things along the same lines that I did. We wouldn't want anybody to be exactly like us, though, would we? It comes down the point that not everybody is the same and there will be things you don't agree with and compromises will have to be made. This was an area that I did not want to compromise. I didn't think it was an area that I should be expected to compromise.

Since Lily had had the same kind of addiction in the past, I sought her viewpoint. She told me that addicts are not able to choose stopping to drink or use a drug of choice. There is something within them that knows it's wrong and knows that they could lose even the things they love the most, but the addiction to whatever it is they might be addicted to is too strong to overcome on their own.

That would lead to the question why wouldn't they seek help? If you knew something could jeopardize the life you're living, why wouldn't you try your best not to let that happen? I think a lot of it is pride. Sometimes you won't even admit to yourself what has happened and what your life has become. And if you won't admit it to yourself, there's no way you'll ever admit it to someone else.

That is probably the part of Brian that didn't understand why he did what he did. He knew he felt awful after a night of partying, but the urge to party had such a strong hold on him he didn't know how to change it. When he was in the midst of partying the last thing on his mind was stopping. All he could do is apologize after a long night of partying. Apologizing to himself as well as to me was all he could do.

I asked Brian once why he couldn't just be himself; the self he was when he woke up in the morning. He would rebut with 'this is me'. What I meant was, the self that he was made as; the self God had made him to be. I don't think that when he was created he was meant to always be in a clouded state of mind. I'm thinking God had a much better purpose for him than he allowed himself to see.

Another thing he loved to say was that God had made marijuana, I supposed he figured then why not 'use' it. My comeback (though I never said it out loud to him) was God also made arsenic, why not try smoking some of that. Just as God created him with a lot more purpose than he was allowing himself to see, I'm sure there are a lot of purposes for marijuana than just getting high.

We had very different views on such substances. I truly believe that money is not the evil of the world; drugs are. They ruin relationships, they ruin dreams, and they ruin lives. Maybe that's why I became so angry. Besides penting everything up inside of me for so long, I saw the drugs, the drinking and Brian (I suppose) as the enemy; the enemy that was ruining the dream I had of a wonderful life with the man I loved.

More than anything I saw the drugs and the drinking as the enemy. They were the evil that was ruining the perfect life we could have together. I added Brian to the mix because he should have been the one that realized the damage he was causing. He should have realized the hurt he was causing within me. That alone should have urged him to change his way of life.

I'm just assuming that if I had a habit that he did not agree with that I would agree to change or at least agree to a compromise. But Brian would never even consider that what he was doing was wrong. There was no other way of seeing it than his view. Why couldn't I just accept him as he was? I guess because I knew there was a different and a better him buried beneath the surface.

Maybe I had held onto the memories that I still had of when I was a child. It almost ruined the life my parents had together. The first time was even before I was born. My mom had served my dad with divorce papers long before I came along and even before my sister who is four years older than me came along.

The thought of not having as stable of childhood that I had upset me. It wasn't always perfect, but there were two parents there to raise us. I suppose I saw at an early age how drinking could cause what looks as a stable relationship not to be so stable after all. No one really knows what is going on beneath the surface in a relationship, any relationship.

I saw the thought that Brian and I could have had so much. I didn't understand why he didn't choose the life I saw in my dreams. You know, the one with a white picket fence and 2 ½ kids. I do realize though that his view of the perfect life was different than mine. His perfect life probably included a wife that did drugs right alongside him; a wife that would actually roll the joint for him.

Why so many people throw away their lives, I'll never understand. But I guess my view of a perfect life was very different than his view of a perfect life. I should have seen a long time ago that our views were very different and he wasn't going to reform his way of thinking to turn his view into my view. It's not fair of me to expect him to change his views for me. Would I like it if he expected the same of me?

I shouldn't have waited and wasted so much time hoping he would change for me. Expecting him to fit into my mold of what I saw as the perfect life. After I had left a friend of mine told me he probably didn't even like himself much. I know Brian would never admit to that, but I think having me gone was a way for him to avoid what he may be feeling inside. Who would want to be reminded every day that they were not living up to someone else's expectations? Especially if he also wasn't living up to his own expectations of himself.

I think there were things neither of us would admit to the other. I look back and realize that I wasn't happy with the way I handled what me and Brian went through together. I would have been happier if I had lived my life the way I chose, hoping I made an impression on him, but not expecting him to change. If he did great, if he didn't I would still be okay.

# Chapter 10: Interfering with Having a Baby [and my dream life]

Many times Brian would tell me that he thought it was time to have Junior as he called him. This was before we ever even talked about marriage. I was just happy that if only in the back of his mind, he was thinking about the future. Since I met him when he was so much younger than I was, I let the pace of our relationship of getting married and having a baby up to him.

Since I was afraid in the beginning that he would be at risk of flight, I didn't want to push anything or any issue within our relationship. I let the fact that he was so much younger than me rule the way I let things slide. Time kept going by, but I wasn't concerned with time or how fast it was passing us by. I was just hanging on to the fact that we were still together.

Brian always told me that he wasn't going to be the one to get up in the middle of the night for a baby. He also told me he would never change a diaper. That sure changes your mind about wanting to have a baby! Maybe it was all just talk from a guy that at that point in time was too young to even think about having a baby with anyone.

It wasn't just his age; it was his lifestyle and his friends. His friends didn't approve of me, what made me think they would approve of him having or starting a family? I knew his friends had a big impact on his life and I didn't want to rock the boat. It was best to lay low and just let things develop slowly.

I did understand that I would be the only one there to take care of the child. But, after all, he was the one bringing home a paycheck and that wasn't left up to me, so I decided to let it slide. When we first moved to Montana, we both worked. Brian was just beginning his business and I got a clerical job at an electronics company. We found a house to move into at that time. A couple years after we moved to Montana, Brian allowed me to quit my job. So in my eyes, having to get up in the night and to be the one that always changed diapers was an even trade.

Some of my friends were concerned that in their eyes the relationship wasn't moving forward. But being good friends as they were, they didn't say anything. It wasn't until after the relationship ended that two of my close friends told me they were so glad that I finally ended it. It kind of made me wonder why they never said anything before that, but I think they knew that I wouldn't have changed things just because they didn't feel the same way that I did.

I think in the same way that Brian's friends didn't like me because they feared I would change him and take him away from them, my friends weren't fond of him because they saw that I was letting go of some of my dreams because of him. I was slowly letting things slide and thinking it was okay if certain things didn't turn out as I had always wanted them to.

I had, like all little girls, dreamed of getting married to a wonderful man who cherished me and having a family with him. As time went by though, my viewpoint of my dreams changed. Within the first couple years I was very concerned we weren't moving towards marriage. In my eyes the years we were together were stacking up though no mention of a long term commitment was mentioned.

I never mentioned anything to Brian. I thought I better just enjoy the time we had together. Maybe it would turn into something long-term. I think I always thought that if I gave it enough time, things would work out for us. Maybe he just needed a little more time to grow up. And if time was what he needed, then I could be patient and wait.

I also was starting to change my mind about marriage. As a kid and a young adult, there was nothing I wanted more than to have a secure place to call my own, but I was realizing this wasn't security. You should have a soft place to land when things in this world go bad or go wrong; you should have somebody to depend on; somebody that you could fall back on and someone you knew would support you.

I think it's ironic that Brian always told me that he saw me and our relationship as a soft place for him to land. He found comfort in knowing he could depend on me. I think he needed that in his life. He needed to know that when there was nothing else out there or nobody else to depend on, he could turn to me. I wanted to be that place for him, though I never even questioned why I couldn't also be able to depend on him and have him be that place for me.

My parents had been married just shy of 50 years when Dad passed away. That's the view of marriage that I had. It wasn't always perfect and sometimes not even very pretty, but they made it through the years together; they worked hard and made it together. Brian's parents divorced when he was very young, so he didn't have a view that had any stability in it.

Sometimes I wonder how two people get together and make it work. Everyone is from such different backgrounds that I do wonder how people come together and compromise along the way. I do know that it takes a lot of compromise from both people. You can't always get what you want and sometimes you have to bend. Sometimes giving will allow you to also get something you value.

And you can't let other people or their opinions get in the way. I'm sure Brian's friends had a lot of opinions about me as well as do his family. My friends didn't let their views be known until after Brian and I broke up. My family was always on our side and always wished us the best.

Maybe deep inside they knew we wouldn't make it, but they never let on to thinking that. They also weren't aware of the challenges we faced together.

Years later, my view was different. I started rethinking how it would be much easier to get out of the relationship if we weren't married. The thoughts of a messy divorce and us battling each other for what we had left was not pleasant. Most people would see that as a bad sign. If you're already thinking of divorce long before you get married, maybe you might want to rethink the marriage. It wasn't that that was my main focus; it was just always in the back of my mind.

And I wasn't always able to depend on Brian. It's hard to be able to depend on someone with a chemical dependency. They can hardly depend on themselves, let alone be there for someone else who is looking to depend on them. Even before I met him, I always knew that I could take care of myself. Maybe I had the same sort of viewpoint as he himself had. That his friends would be his friends long after I was gone, and I knew I'd still be okay even after he was gone as I was always able to take care of myself.

I started to think about the fact of how hard it would be to get out of a marriage. Lily got married and it took her years to be able to get out of that because her ex-husband decided not to cooperate much. I didn't see Brian being like that, but things could get messy and I didn't want to have to deal with that. I still held on to the hope I always had that he would see the errors of his way and change.

There were times I got angry because according to me he wasn't playing the game according to my rules! If he would stop being so stubborn, things would roll along smoothly and we would end up being happy. I didn't think I was asking more of him than he could give. But it wasn't a game, now was it? It was just that we had different views of life. I think in the beginning we had the same view of a life together, but somewhere along the way, it took different turns than we expected.

I think that's where the compromise would have or should have come in. Somewhere along the line, someone has to compromise. I think we thought we both compromised where we could, but in the end maybe we didn't compromise enough. I didn't think I could compromise to the point he wanted. I had very different views of where I drew the line when it came to substance abuse and I probably pushed it further than I wanted to. It just wasn't okay with me to live the way he was living.

I believed I had the power to change things for him as well as for us as a couple. All codependents feel they have that power within them. They hold on to that thought. They want to believe that the love the other person feels for you will be enough to cause them to change. You want to believe that the fear of losing you will be enough to cause the other to change their ways. It's not. It should be, but it's not. The chemicals that the person is addicted to are so much more powerful than the love or actions of any person. That's the sad part.

# Chapter 11: Taking Care of Myself

There were many times I almost left. There was always something that stopped me, though. There was the love I felt for him, as well as the love I knew he felt for me. He would always tell me he loved me dearly. I always thought I was what was holding him together and if I left who knows where that would leave him. The guilt I felt or thought I would feel was unbearable.

Maybe that was because Brian did always tell me he would fall apart if I ever left. I believed him. How would he be able to take care of himself? For so many years, I was the one that took care of him. I was the one that kept everything together. I was the one that paid all the bills, made dinner and held us together. I was the one he depended upon. How would he survive without me? How would he be able to steer his life, to guide his life, without having me behind the steering wheel? What would he do without the direction I supplied? He even made me promise once that I would never leave him. So I did.

That, of course, had a lot to do with the codependency I held within. I felt and believed I was the only one that could help Brian live his life the way he should. I knew best. The frustration came when he would not listen to the valuable information I had. When you think someone should listen to you and be thankful for the guidance you are trying to give but they are not thankful, they are actually bitter for the invasion you create you yourself become angry; angry that your guidance is not being adhered to and accepted.

I became angry. So angry I did not know what to do with the feelings I held inside. So, I pounded on walls and doors, threw a picture frame at Brian's feet (only once) and slept on the couch or in the other bedroom a lot. Mostly the nights he stayed out at the bars, which became more frequent before I left.

After I left, I learned that Brian's sister and her new boyfriend went to Montana. She took my place in taking care of him by grocery shopping for him. Brian still didn't have to deal with everyday life on his own. The fall was cushioned so he still didn't have to go about life on his own. In a way it made me feel better knowing he was taken care of, even if I had to admit I wasn't the only one who could fill those shoes.

What I did not understand at that time was that I did not have the right (or the power) to lead Brian's life for him. I am only responsible for myself and my own life and no one else's. I can only be who I am and I have to let others be who they are. And I am not responsible for the choices Brian makes. I can give my suggestions and my point of view but that's as far as I can go. Ultimately, he is responsible for the choices he makes and if they turn out to be wrong or bad choices, he is the one that must deal with the consequences.

That is not an easy thing to do. To sit back and watch as someone makes the decisions that in time will harm him or make it so he has hard consequences to live with. That is the one thing my sister always worried about. Since Brian had built a strong business since we moved to Montana, she worried that his lifestyle and choices would not only jeopardize the life he had created for himself but the one he had created for me also, the one that included the both of us. The life that we had together could be changed because of the poor choices he made even if I had nothing to do with that way of life he lived. The human tendency in all of us wants to protect and to shield the other.

It happened not long after we moved to Montana, not long after September 11$^{th}$ 2001 took place. One of the things that were stressed in the news was placing a large amount of stamps on an envelope. Brian's one friend wasn't that smart. Not to mention sending drugs through the United States Postal Service isn't smart, putting a large amount of stamps on an envelope at that time wasn't either.

To remind Brian of that, we received a visit from six law officers one evening in November. It was an unpleasant experience I thought I'd never have to live through. I did not live my life where cops stormed into my house. I know Brian wouldn't agree with my words in that last sentence, but to me, not having lived that lifestyle, it was traumatic. I never had a boyfriend that I had to watch be handcuffed. I never was questioned the way the officers questioned me. After that, I had become quite familiar with the law enforcement within our area.

The good thing was they came to find out that I had nothing to do with that way of life. I'm embarrassed to say I put a lot of four letter words in a journal I kept at the time. When they came to the house that November evening, they found my journal and confiscated it. I still to this day have not gotten that journal back.

At the same time, I didn't want to do anything that caused Brian to have to pay. But I also wanted the police to know I wasn't like that, that I took no part in that lifestyle. And they learned that. They learned that from talking to me outside and once they hauled Brian off to jail we moved inside where they continued to search the house thinking he stashed drugs inside. There were never any drugs inside the house. Brian knew better than to do that.

They learned about me from the journal I had been keeping that they found. I kept a journal that was originally supposed to be what is called 'Morning Pages' that had to do with my writing. Those kinds of pages didn't last long for they soon turned into pages that held my feelings about drugs and what Brian was involving himself in. There were many colorful four letter words that were the only way for me to express my feelings and my viewpoint on what he did and how he lived. I suppose in a way that made me feel safe. Safe that Brian and I would be spared because the law officers knew that I had nothing to do with the drugs. That maybe they would find mercy on us because of the goodness they saw in me.

I thought it would get better after that. But nothing ever happened from that encounter. Not that I wanted him to, but Brian was never prosecuted at all for that incident or anything else because of that. Earlier the next year, he also got into trouble when he went to visit his friend in Vermont. His sister went with him that year. They drove across country to visit. They had a large amount of marijuana with them at that time too. They were in Ohio where his mom lived.

I don't know the whole story behind it, but I know that he took full responsibility so his sister would not get in trouble. They also got lucky when pulled over in New York for a speeding ticket. He did have to go back to Ohio though when his court case came about. He got off of that on a technicality, which I don't even know the whole of that story either. There were a lot of cases like that in Brian's life. I never wanted him to get in trouble. I just wished he would learn his lesson, though not by going to jail. Even though he would get in trouble and had to pay a lot of money he never did learn his lesson, at least not while I was there.

Jail came later, though I was gone and living in Arizona. It was actually not long after I left, and was one of the times he stopped by to see me while in town. He was in town to pick up another load (sorry I'm not sure what you call it) of marijuana. He got caught again while in Idaho. According to him, he got pulled over for the window tint being too dark and the police officer asked him to open his trunk. That's when he looked in the cooler that Brian had filled up with marijuana.

That's the time he left Arizona and he would usually call me when he got back home to Montana. We still had a close relationship and we still cared for each other. I knew that type of lifestyle that he led, so I was always worried about him for that reason. He disappeared for days. I even called his sister and she had no idea where he was.

I even called a friend of his in Montana because I knew she was taking care of our dog. I thought she might have heard from him or knew where he was. She told me that he was having 'family problems' as she called it. I knew that was a lie because I had talked to his sister and even she did not know where he was.

I heard from him a few days later at 1:30 a.m. He had gotten home, but he was angry I called his friend. I tried to explain that I was worried if my dog was taken care of or not. By the end of the phone call he seemed to calm down and apologized for calling at the time he called at.

I still don't know if he learned from that incident. I guess going to jail is just one of the hazards of that lifestyle. If they are caught, they just learn to do it better next time as to not get caught. He would never let his true feelings out as to how he felt regarding any of these incidents. I guess being a guy means never letting anyone see your true feelings or that you might be frightened. That would mean coming across as weak.

After those few incidents, I hoped that he learned something. I knew he would never tell me how he truly felt or if he changed. I held on to that hope, but it was never proved to me either way. All a girl can do is hope. It's not that I wanted to be right; I just wanted him to change his ways to see that there is a better way to live.

# Chapter 12: A Blessing –
# Having Lily in My Life

I believe people are brought into your life for a reason. That's one reason why I did not want to let go of Brian. We were brought into each other's life for a reason. Being a true codependent, I believed it was for his benefit; for the sole reason of me being able to help him 'get better'. Every person, though, has to decide for him or herself what they do with their life and the lessons that are placed in front of them.

And now I see how selfish it was on my part. I didn't trust his view of the world because I knew drugs tainted his sight. As I mentioned before, it wasn't right of me to expect him to conform to my ways. He has a right to his views and his way of life. I think I wasted a lot of energy on trying to prove I was right, at least in my eyes. He, of course, didn't see my ways as being right, at least not for him.

I did believe I could help Brian and that is what drove me to behave the way I did; but because of the way I was behaving that forced him to build a wall. I am not placing blame on him; I am just trying to understand my actions. I loved him so much I couldn't stand to watch the destructive behavior and the consequences it brought. I, too, though had a lot to learn.

For a long time, I believed that only I knew what was best for Brian. I knew how he should change, I knew how he should live his life and I knew what was best for him. Oh, us codependents! We just figure that by changing things the way we see fit that will help the other and make a better world for both them and us. We believe we have all the answers if only anyone would listen.

Anger consumes you slowly. The kind of anger that is associated with not being able to control a situation like you would like to be able to control it; not being able to understand how someone can be controlled by a substance; and not being able to understand why they choose not to change.

As Lily explained to me, it is a force that holds so tight the person has a hard time changing. Besides Brian thinking that he was not wrong in the way that he was thinking, the substance had a hold on him that he couldn't shake. The easiest thing for him was to just give in to the substance.

The anger like I felt does no one any good. It does not help the situation. The other person is not going to 'change' because they do not want to see you get as angry as you do. It only places stress on the relationship. It will make them angry also. People do not like to be controlled. I mean, would I?

If you look at the situation and put yourself in the place of another, you wouldn't like it if someone were trying to control you the same way either. Codependents are not able to put themselves in the addict's situation, though, because they, of course, cannot understand how anyone can be controlled by something like a substance. But they still know that they wouldn't like it if someone were trying to control them.

Logically I knew that, but logic is not something that takes precedence in a situation like this. Your whole focus is on getting the other person to stop doing the things that are harming them. The first obstacle is getting them to see the harm in it all. Just as anyone would have a hard time convincing me that my views were wrong, any person dependent on any substance is also going to view his way of thinking as right.

I now understand that Brian didn't see what he was doing as harmful to himself. I do think he regrets harming me and my feelings, but I feel that worse than he does. He did not want to put pressure on me, but he also did not see what he was doing as 'wrong'. I was the one putting pressure on him. I was the one insistent on him changing his way of thinking. In my eyes at the time, I was doing it out of love. I was trying to protect him.

Lily has been a true blessing in my life. She has helped me understand things that I would not have understood if it hadn't been for her being placed in my life at the time she was placed there. I admit I didn't always agree with her philosophy because we were coming from different perspectives, but I did understand that she told me the things she told me out of love.

It took me a long time to admit that I knew she was right, that she held the key to my understanding my own problem. I would be in a worse position if I hadn't had Lily in my life. I would have been on my own trying to understand an area I cannot understand and feeling even worse than I did at the time.

Before we moved to Montana Lily asked me if I thought that would change things. Of course, it would I said. It will be better because his friends would be 1200 miles away and I would have more influence over him instead of the drinking and drugs. Lily laughed because she knew all too well that the distance wouldn't matter. As I stated before, they make new friends.

Looking back now, I wish I had listened to my friend. Of course she knew what she was talking about. I honestly believed that our love would be strong enough to change things for the better. I thought eventually it would take hold of Brian and he would change. It might have been better to hope it took hold of me, which it eventually did, but not before we both suffered emotional loss.

I tried my best to fill Brian's life with other things. We went to a local garden shop and planted a flower garden out front at our new house. A lot of the time we would go four-wheeling because I knew Brian loved that and at the same time we would take our dog for a run. The dog loved chasing the truck or running along side of it as we drove around the wooded areas.

But I held on to the hope that Brian would come to understand the wrongs of his ways. I finally came to the conclusion that that was the old codependent me that for so long still clung to the hope that Brian and I were destined to be together. There is also and will always be the part of me that wants what is best for Brian; the part of me that doesn't want his life to one full of court dates, jail time and pain.

I do know, though sometimes struggle against, the knowledge that everything happens in its own time frame. Everything has a season according to God's plan. It is sometimes hard to wait for the good. I am an extremely impatient person and that may just be my lesson. I need to understand the art of waiting. Everything in good time.

# *Chapter 13: Leaving*

This is the hardest chapter to write. It reminds me of what I could have changed. If I did, I wonder if we'd still be together. And I used to beat myself up with the 'what if's'. In the back of my mind I think if I had just done this or just done that maybe I'd still be there, maybe we'd still be together. Maybe if we had just worked a little harder we would still be together. Though it would have to have been a decision we both came to not just me.

Though I hate to admit it, this day was coming for a long time. I had known for quite a while that something in this relationship probably wasn't right. I chose to ignore it though. I didn't want to let go of the love that I had found; the love that I thought was forever. We had even talked about forever. Nobody wants to let go of something like that.

I never meant to hurt Brian. I think I did, though he would probably never admit it. I never hated him; I never wished bad things on him. I was as hurt and frustrated as I'm sure he was. I was to the point that I didn't know what else to do, how else to solve the situation. I came to the conclusion that something was guiding me; something was helping me to see a way out of all the hurt we had created within the relationship.

I didn't plan the move out. It came about one evening because of the anger I felt that revolved around one specific evening. It was the circumstances of that evening that pushed me to start packing. Brian was again at the local bar without telling me or asking me to join him.

Something propelled me to go looking for him and I found him. I came in and sat next to him. I did take notice that the bar was very crowded, packed actually, but that didn't seem to deter us from getting into a horrendous fight right there in the middle of the bar. When I came in I noticed that the guy sitting next to him patted him on the back as if to say' sorry she found you.'

I didn't even have a chance to order a drink when he got mad at something I said. Sadly, I can't even remember what started the fight now. He got up to leave so I followed. I said if you're leaving then so am I. He said if I was leaving he'd stay, if not he was leaving alone.

I proceeded to follow him to the other room of the bar where we continued yelling at each other. I followed him outside where we continued to fight. I tried to give the free drink tokens I had back to him and he wouldn't take them. Something within me got very angry when he refused to let me stay or to have a decent evening together. He mentioned something about me causing a scene or something, so I threw the tokens at him that I had brought with me and said you want to see a scene then here you go as I proceeded to floor my car and squeal out of the back parking lot.

After I left the bar parking lot, I went back to our house. I don't think the scene we just caused even fazed me. I'm not one to even stand up in a crowd, so what just happened didn't even set in to my consciousness for quite a while. I wasn't embarrassed or anything, I was just so full of rage and anger that I completely didn't even acknowledge that we were in a public place that was actually very crowded. The fact that he wouldn't even talk to me about anything angered me. I just wanted him to listen and understand my point of view.

I didn't think he would be home for quite a while after that. I was still so angry I came home, went into the garage and found boxes in the rafters. I dragged them out, brought them into the house and went into the kitchen, grabbed some old newspapers and started to pack the kitchen plates and dishes. At the time, that made me feel better. I still had so much anger inside though.

It was comforting to be home with my animals. You can't ever do anything wrong that will make a dog or a cat look at you differently. They are filled with unconditional love. So the dog and cat just sat there watching me pack dishes into boxes. I know they didn't understand or even wonder why I brought the boxes in or why I was putting the dishes in a box.

That night I slept in the other bedroom, which is something I had been doing quite often. Either the other bedroom or the couch was where I slept the majority of the time. At that point his going out drinking and staying out was a common thing. I would still wake up when he got home even if I wasn't sleeping in our bedroom, but I could avoid the sounds of his deep snoring because of his drinking that would happen later as he fell asleep.

I didn't sleep that well that night. As the hours passed, I tried not to worry about Brian. It was just the usual feeling. Knowing he was out drinking and worrying about him and if he would make it home was familiar. The morning came, but Brian didn't. I went about showering and the usual routine I had. At 9:30 a.m. the phone rang. It was Brian saying he was on his way and asking if I'd be home. Of course, I would I said. So, I waited for him to come home.

He arrived home shortly before 10:15 a.m. After he came in, he came over to the couch I was sitting on. He lay down with his head on my lap. "I don't know why I do what I do," he said. I remember running my fingers through his hair. He was just a helpless little boy in my lap; one that I wanted so much to rescue and help.

It made me sad to not being able to understand why we were living through what we were living through. But if he didn't understand why, how could I think I could understand? I suppose as you're drinking rationality leave you. You don't think about what you should do or why. Common sense goes out the window.

He said he was hungry, so I offered to go to the local Subway just up the street. I left to get lunch and that's when he discovered that most of the kitchen was not in the cupboards any more. This is another area I beat myself up over. What if I had just unpacked after that day? What if I never had packed at all? What if we had just sat down and talked about things? But we didn't. After I got back from Subway, I recall him asking where all the dishes were. I told him I was very hurt after the incident in the bar. I don't recall us talking any further about it though.

He didn't go out all night for almost a week later, but eventually he started again. We never talked about anything like we should have. I do wonder why we never sat down and talked anything out. Maybe it wouldn't have changed anything, but at least we would have tried. Looking back, I feel like I failed. I knew we didn't give it our all. I felt like we hadn't even really tried.

After that evening, I just remember packing more. It's like I heard my own voice (or someone's voice) telling me, warning me not to waste any more time. That's another area I beat myself up over. Why did I continue packing my belongings? And whose voice was that? Whatever or who's ever voice that was, I didn't question it. I trusted that it was guiding me in the right direction.

So it was that something inside of me that propelled me to keep packing, some unseen force. And something inside of me said if I left this would make it better. I believed that to be telling me that things would get better for Brian and me – together. Maybe it was just saying things would get better for us – even if it meant separately. But at the time I couldn't even think about the possibility of that scenario.

They say God works in mysterious ways. Maybe this is one of those ways. I finally realized for my own sanity and Brian's too this was the best thing at least for the time being. We were hurting each other in ways we didn't want to. He claimed it was me who pushed him to drink and do drugs.

As I mentioned earlier, you alone never have the power to control someone else's life like that. It is a choice they make that has nothing to do with you. I've learned from my studies of codependency that your feelings and reactions are never another person's fault. You are responsible for your own thoughts, feeling and actions. I knew that it just made him feel better to be able to cast the blame on another, for him to blame me. It helped for him to believe that it wasn't his fault; that it was mine.

I do believe that everything works out as it should and for the best. The moment you realize that though could be long in coming. I didn't want to hurt and I didn't want Brian to hurt. That wasn't my intention. My intention at the time was to stop hurting; to stop being a doormat for the emotional abuse.

My intention was to fix the relationship, to fix both of us. We instilled hurt in each other that takes time to heal. Now I realize there were better ways to go about it. This is where the beating myself up comes in too. But who's to say that the same kind of hurt wouldn't be taking place if I had stayed. I needed to take care of myself and this was apparently how I was supposed to do it. Not that I didn't go kicking and screaming along the road I was placed on, but this was obviously something I needed to do.

# Chapter 14: How I Wanted to Be There to Pick Up the Pieces When He Fell

Now I'm not saying that Brian is destined to 'crash'. I always thought he could take care of himself. Well, that isn't exactly truth. There were times I thought (and other people said to me) that he couldn't do this by himself. I spent so many years taking care of him how could he take care of himself? How would he manage? He depended so much on me to take care of and handle everything.

But he is a big boy after all, so who's to say it would end badly I thought? Maybe he won't fall and stumble at all. Maybe the sheer determination will keep him afloat. There are also all the people helping him. Maybe because they worry about him like I do; maybe because they care about him just like I do.

The ride down here was like a vacation to me. It was fun. I was carefree and refused to acknowledge why we were driving down to Arizona. It was just a good time; one where we enjoyed each other's company. He seemed a bit more subdued. It was as if he knew and was thinking about why we were driving and where we were driving to.

It was strange the way things had changed. We had broken up several times before we called it quits. At the time, I had a very hard time at first and Brian was just fine. As time went on, I felt stronger and Brian seemed to falter. It was as if he suddenly realized what he had walked away from. After I had walked away and moved back to Arizona, I changed my mind not long after that.

We are still friends and I do care about him deeply. I mean, how can you not after you spent nine years with someone? The first year after I left, not more than two weeks went by where Brian and I didn't speak. He started calling me and keeping in touch with me more than I called him. Then it switched to me calling him more often. Brian seemed to have a hard time with things at first and then he slowly let go. I was okay at first, but as time went by, I began to have a hard time.

Of course, then came the time that I was the one falling apart. Only three months had passed and I wanted nothing more than to go home to his warm, safe arms. I had intended on spending forever with him and I couldn't believe that I was the one who decided that forever would suddenly end. So, I called him up asking to come home. He got very angry with me that night. He said no more times than I could count. I continued to beg and cry. After almost an hour of going back and forth, he hung up on me.

I proceeded to cry – I mean hysterically cry – to him and tell him that I wanted to come home. I was tired of being without him and tired of being alone. I was tired of having to deal with life alone. Life was just too hard without him. Everything comes crashing at you and you have no one to lean on or who will buffer the throws that life casts at you.

I remember going to bed completely numb. The kind of numb that had become familiar to me. It was the same numb I felt within the couple days we spent packing me up and driving down here. I refused to focus on the fact that this was the end of our relationship. I went through the motions of packing up all my stuff without even thinking about the why.

Then he called me the very next night. He said he would like a thirty-day reprieve on his answer. Still feeling numb, I didn't want to push, so I just said okay. But the thirty days turned into 60, 120, and 280. Being as I didn't want to push I left it alone. Somewhere around the 150 days I began to question my own sanity; not only the sanity (or insanity) of going back to a life like that, but of being so passive as to let him walk all over me again. I didn't want to rock the boat so I kept quiet.

So, I called him one day telling him that his 30-day reprieve turned into almost 180 days, he laughed. That should have been another clue. But things were hard. Things were hard alone and they weren't getting better. Not that I couldn't take care of myself, I've done it before for a long time. But having known the security of being a couple, I didn't want to be alone. I thought I found someone I was going to spend forever with; I didn't want to give that security up.

We are still friends and I do care about him deeply. I mean, how can you not after you spent nine years with someone? The first year after I left, not more than two weeks went by where Brian and I didn't speak. He started calling me and keeping in touch with me more than I called him. Then it switched to me calling him more often. Brian seemed to have a hard time with things at first and then he slowly let go. I was okay at first, but as time went by, I began to have a hard time.

I didn't want to lose him as a friend either. We had been through so much together. There were both good and bad memories. I wanted to hang on to the good. I wanted to create more good and I knew we could if given the chance. Being a very stubborn person (not to mention codependent) I was convinced that I could convince him and change his mind. Though I was also convinced I could convince him to stop doing drugs and drinking like he was and that hadn't worked.

But I also realized that some people never change. And when I learned more about codependency I also learned that if people are going to change it can't be because another person 'forced' them into their way of thinking. Everyone has to make their own decisions in their own time. I may not like the fact I can't control circumstances like I thought I could, but over time, acceptance of that fact made life easier.

That was a hard one for me to take hold of. I still had the mindset that I knew best for Brian. The way I saw it was Brian couldn't make his own decisions – at least not the right ones. I, of course, knew what was best for the both of us. I just knew we could have a very happy life together as we had been having, but drugs would have to leave the scenario within his life.

I understood the concept of codependency and how you can't change other people, I just didn't like it. I wanted him to listen to me and I wanted him to do what I wanted him to do. That's the controlling part of codependency. It's not that we don't care about the other person, it's that we care too much and in the wrong way. The other part of the jigsaw puzzle that is missing is the caring about ourselves.

If we can't take care of ourselves, no one else will. Being codependent we do think there would be someone there to pick up the pieces like I did for Brian, but the thought of someone trying to control me would drive me crazy. As it did Brian. Who could blame him for getting so angry with me?

The truth is you teach people how to treat you. If you continue to be a punching bag, not literally but figuratively, for someone, of course they're going to continue to treat you like they do. They know they can get away with it, right? And you can't change what you don't acknowledge. Even if we learn to live with it, we shouldn't. We need to learn we can't control someone else; we can only control our own lives.

If we don't take care of ourselves, we won't be any good to care for others. If you aren't well yourself, how can you help others? And I don't mean care for others in the codependent sort of way. I mean care for others, as you would care for a friend or relative.

You can't care about someone if you are not well. It wreaks havoc on a body, on a family, on a situation. No one will be any better for it. And once we start caring for ourselves we might just be a little more sane and able to handle situations without flying off the handle. Understanding we can't control others, brings a sort of peace within our lives.

If I had taken care of myself first, Brian and I might not have been in the situation we found ourselves in. It wasn't his fault and it wasn't my fault. It was a situation that neither one of us knew how to handle, and, honestly, we handled it badly. They say hindsight is twenty-twenty. Isn't that the truth? Though I'm not sure what we could have changed within those circumstances or even wanted to.

We were both stubborn and didn't want to conform to the other's lifestyle because the lives we lead were so different in contrast to each other. They say opposites attract, but do they attract for the right reasons? Maybe we just weren't suited for each other. I know everyone has to work on relationships, but you shouldn't have to work that hard in a relationship. In the end maybe it was best just to let it go.

# Chapter 15: I Still Had Hopes it Would Work Out

When I first started writing this book, I started this chapter titled, *I Still Have Hopes It Will Work Out*. I held on to that for many years. As I mentioned, that first year Brian and I talked every week. It was just like I was on vacation. The thought that this was permanent were buried deep within my mind.

Maybe in the back of my mind I was hoping it wouldn't work out for Brian. That he would not be able to take care of himself. That he would miss me so much that he would throw in the towel and the white flag would come up. I spent so long taking care of him, how could he survive without me? I honestly didn't want things to go badly for him. I just didn't want to be alone.

Funny how codependents think they have the ability to run someone else's life, but don't control their own very well. It's not that we aren't capable of controlling our own lives; it's that we have learned to focus on other people's lives. We learn to ignore our own lives and our own needs. Other people in our lives are just more important to us than ourselves.

When we put someone else in front of ourselves, we put what is happening in our own lives behind everything else. What is happening in our lives isn't as important as fixing everyone else's lives to the point we think they should be fixed. We are convinced we know how to run our own lives; other people just don't know how to run theirs.

What I wanted was for Brian was to realize that the life he is leading isn't the way to go. Here comes my codependent side again. I want him to realize that life is so much better and easier when it is 'unfogged' and when it is done while 'straight' without the use of drugs. To me, that was an easy decision. Unable to understand his views made it hard for me when I couldn't change those views.

Life is hard enough to deal with sometimes. I think that's what he thinks too, though. That smoking pot and drinking makes it easier. He told me once that that is the way he relaxes. Kind of the way I watch television after a long day. It's just a different kind of relaxing. One's illegal and one's not.

I still saw how happy we could be if he just saw things my way and changed. I know I had no right to expect that from him. He could probably say the same thing about me. If I had just lightened up, it could have worked for us. I'm sure he also thought if I conformed to his way of life or just had accepted it, we would still be together.

I think that too. But drug abuse is just something I couldn't accept. I knew there was a better way. And I knew that from experience. It was always an easy choice for me. Why would you want to live that kind of life, why would you want to not have control over your life? Just by watching the news I knew that that was the case for so many.

I wanted Brian to want me more than I thought he showed. When I said I was going to leave I wanted him to beg me not to go, I wanted him to say he was sorry; that he would change. Instead he held the door open for me. I suppose my little plan backfired. Maybe it was just a game my codependent side played because it thought it would get its way. It never saw the other side of how this could and did end up as.

When I would say that I just wanted him to choose me, he always said he did. I didn't see it like that. I wanted him to choose me over drugs, so when or if I gave an ultimatum that it was the drugs or me; I wanted him to say it's you. I chose you. He didn't. Even though it was an ultimatum sort of situation, he still chose the drugs over being with me.

He could say the same thing, though. I had a choice of accepting him the way he was or leaving. I just didn't see my life the way it turned out. I loved him so much, but I didn't see my life as being entwined with someone who, in my view, was addicted to drugs and that sort of lifestyle. I was always a 'good girl', so why would I choose to end up in this sort of relationship?

It got to the point before I left that we had so much anger built up inside that we didn't spend much time together. He says that I made it impossible on him to the point that he didn't want to come home, so he didn't. I saw it as a substance abuse problem that he was addicted to going out and getting drunk or going out and using drugs, not because of me, but in spite of me. There are always two sides to a story though.

I thought if I shared part of his lifestyle, we could come back together. I was always very anti-drug but drinking (as long as you can handle it and didn't go over board) was okay. We went to the bar many nights, just had a few drinks and would come home. I would make dinner for us and we would have a nice evening. I thought if I showed him how life could be, he would see the good in that.

I once saw a saying that said you have to let go of things to make room for something new. I didn't really want new, I just wanted improved. I wanted things fixed to my satisfaction. I just wanted my life to go as I always dreamed it would. But it is not within my timeframe, it is within God's.

There were so many signs that I chose to either ignore or to make excuses for. But then came the thoughts that I know I needed to go because maybe something 'bad' has to happen before he finally 'gets' it. I have always been there for him to pick up the pieces. Even his mom and aunt have called me an enabler.

If there's always someone to pick up the pieces and make everything better, how is he ever going to learn? And that's something I did all the time. I cleaned up the messes he created. When he got in trouble, I bailed him out. It's just something you do without even thinking about it when you love somebody.

Like I said before every lesson in each individual's time and in his or her own way. In everybody's life, things will work out the way they are meant to. Sitting back and watching is hard though. Maybe that's why I always opted to help. I felt he didn't know how to do it right, so I would show him.

So, in my own way, I was just trying to teach him. I thought if I showed him how easy life could be he would choose me and the lifestyle I was creating for him. All I had to do, in my eyes, was make his life easier for him and he would follow. That, though, is not up to me.

That's a lesson in itself for me to learn. It was a lesson I had to learn about letting people live their lives on their own. Whether it works out as I think it should or not. There are probably people out there who don't believe in the way I live my life. Brian would probably be one of those people. He would probably see my life as boring and not much fun.

I guess that's what makes life, well life. Not everyone has the same views. So everyone's experience is different. We all have free will. We all have the capability of choosing. There are rules of right and wrong whether we follow them or not. The end result is the result we end up living with.

For each of us, it will either work out or it won't. According to our own choices, we create our own lives. So maybe there is someone else out there waiting for me and I had to give up the present to get a better future. It took a lot for me to change things, though. It took me awhile to get rolling on the life that could be.

And it took me a long time to learn I couldn't control Brian's life. I finally saw that things were not working as I wanted them to. In the back of my mind, I knew I was wrong. I knew that things had to change. For not only my sake, but for Brian's too.

It's a hard lesson either way, but one I know I am getting better at each and every day. It wasn't easy at first, but it gets easier as the days go by. It was a lesson I had to learn in my own time. I had to learn when to walk away. It wasn't giving up, it was just letting go of my view of how Brian's life should be.

Besides knowing that I don't have much of a choice, I want what's best for both of us and maybe that isn't having the other or being in each other's lives. I had to learn strength. I know I had strength within; I just had to figure out how to let it surface.

I came across a verse one day that said 'Trust and Let Go'. 'Let go and let God'. I've tried to live by that. It is hard to let go though, that I admit. You have to trust God and know that all will work out as it should. There came another situation that I had a hard time letting go of too.

# Chapter 16: The Day Something 'Bad' Came (Jail)

I knew Brian came down to Arizona every February. It was javelina hunting time and Brian and his friends always went. The year after I left I expected him to be in Arizona in February and after the hunt he did call. We went out for pizza and had a nice time together. What I didn't expect was for him to come back the next month.

I called him one evening but he said he was busy and would call me back. He called me the next day around 5:00. He said he had just gotten off work. After about 25 minutes on the phone, I asked him, shouldn't you be home by now? He started talking about all the construction around Polson, the next town over from where we lived. So, I thought nothing else of it.

Around 3:00 a.m. the following morning I received a phone call from him. He said he needed a place to stay and could he stay with me? I asked him where he was and he said, I'm pulling into your driveway. I looked out the window and sure enough, he was pulling into the parking lot. It was quite a surprise. So, I let him in.

He had driven straight through from Montana, he said. When I had called him the previous day, he was somewhere around Salt Lake City. He claimed, technically, he had never said he was back in Montana.

Maybe not, but he could have told me he was heading towards me. Maybe he wouldn't have even called me if he had gone straight to his sister's house. She lives another hour from me and he was too beat to drive that at three in the morning. So I let him sleep. He left around 7:00 a.m. I had a job where I did not have a set hour that I had to be there, so it was okay if I showed up around 8:00.

There was another time back in November that he had come here but never told me. I found out because I received the cell phone bill. It had always been in my name and after we switched it to Brian's name, I received one last bill. The only thing it had on it though, was roaming charges and the dates in November that he was here. He never called me that time.

I knew why he was here, but since I didn't want to be judgmental, I didn't say anything about it. I knew though that he had come to pick up another (shipment/load/batch) of marijuana. I wished he would stop doing that. He had told me years ago that he was going to stop. At that time, he obviously hadn't stopped.

He told me he might come back so he could leave early Sunday morning because he had to be back for some jobs on Monday. I knew he was with his friends that evening, so the chances he would come back were slim. He called me early Sunday at 6:00 a.m. and said he was sorry he hadn't come back but it was late Saturday night and he stayed at his sister's so he could sleep a little. He called me again at 10:00 just to talk. The last thing I said to him was please call when you get home so I know you're safe. He always called when he got home. He called me when I lived with him and he went down to Arizona and he called me when I didn't live with him and he got back home. So, when he didn't call me that night or the next morning, I knew something was wrong.

I called his cell phone over and over, but he never answered, nor did he call me back. I called his brother-in-law, and I called his sister on Monday evening, but no one had heard from him or knew where he was. The first thing I always think of was an accident. I admit it;

I'm a worrier. For some reason, I always think of the worst situation possible.

His sister said that his friend, Charlie, had called him and some other guy answered the phone. Charlie got freaked out and hung up. So, that led me to believe (as my crazy thinking goes) that someone hurt him and had his cell phone. The other thought was that he was in jail. That might be why he didn't have his cell phone and was not able to call me back. I didn't understand why someone else would answer his phone though. Would one of the police officers actually answer it? I didn't think so, but maybe they did.

I was encouraged when his sister told me the next day that Brian had called her asking for a friend of theirs phone number in Phoenix. She said he didn't say much else that was all he needed. At least I was encouraged that he was alive and well. It still didn't explain much though. Then Wednesday morning he called me at 1:30 a.m. He was angry that I called his family and worried them and he was mad I called a female friend of his to inquire about him and my dog back in Montana. I explained that I did because I was worried because he didn't call like he always did when he got home. He did calm down and said he was sorry he woke me up and to go back to sleep.

He ended up calling me a week later and confessed that he was in jail. I told him I already knew that. When he gets angry at me and comes unglued as he did and yells at me like he did, it's a clear sign that he's angry because I figured him out and knew exactly what was going on. He explained how much money he had to pay ($8,000 to retain the attorney) not to mention the money he owed his friend for the drugs he had taken that the cops now had. He mentioned $10,000. I knew from when he was doing this when I lived with him that he owed his friend $5,000 for what he got back then. I didn't want to think about how much he had gotten caught with.

He kept telling me that he could have to spend a year in jail if he was convicted and that I may have to move back for that time. It wasn't for several months that I found out his attorney told him the maximum sentence was 22 years! Now, I obviously don't agree with the lifestyle that he led but 22 years? That seemed extreme to me. There are rapists and child molesters you hear of that barely get four years if even and they let them out. Yes, he had a substantially large amount of marijuana, but that just didn't seem right to me.

His attorney wasn't very good at keeping in touch either. Brian said he had talked to him once when he first retained him. He got him out of the first hearing and he was supposed to drag it out as long as he could so Brian could work throughout the summer. When I talked to Brian in early June he said he had gotten something in the mail that said he had a pre-trial hearing on June 6th and the trial would be June 29th. I started getting worried that if they were going to put him away for a while, would they let him return home and just expect him to return to carry his sentence out or would they take him right there and then on that day? And if they did, how would I know? Who would tell me? In the end, Brian had to serve two months in jail. He postponed it until January 2006. He called me several times while in jail. The first time was the very first day he went. Even though they were collect calls, I couldn't turn my back on him and not accept them. After he got out, he did pay me back for all the calls.

Brian claimed that he probably wouldn't have to serve the whole two months. Every few weeks he would call. I always accepted the collect phone calls. Close to the two month time frame after I hadn't heard from him, I called him at our home. A girl answered the phone. I assumed it was his niece. I called throughout the day and the same girl answered; soon after I got a call from that girl. We had caller id in our house so I'm sure my number came up and she called me. She claimed to be his fiancé. She claimed to have an engagement ring on her finger. Thinking back, that would explain why she always answered the phone; because she lived there.

After being on the phone with her, I couldn't believe I was being pulled into this drama, so I hung up on her. Not long after that, Brian's sister called me. She told me that Brian was still in jail and I shouldn't be calling this girl. She told me she was in charge of all his bills, everything until he got out. It was best not to make her angry. This girl told his sister that I was the one that called her! I admit I called looking for Brian, but she was the one who called me back. His sister did tell me this girl was quite the drama queen, but more importantly she was a bold faced liar!

On top of all that, Brian had outright lied to me too. He claimed he didn't know this girl very well. Funny, how can you not know someone who you asked to marry very well? I knew Brian well enough to know two things about him for sure. One, he didn't want to grow old. And two, he didn't want to be alone. It then made so much sense to me. He had once even called me and told me I was his 'ace in the hole'. He had asked her to marry him, but just in case she wasn't there when he got out of jail, he wanted to make sure I was, so he continued to call me from jail. That way he would be assured to have one of us. Did I feel like a fool for falling for his lie? Of course, I did.

He continued to lie to me the whole two months he was in jail. He lied about her and how serious their relationship was. He lied about the engagement ring. I told him when he called once that she says she has an engagement ring on her finger from you. He laughed and said she might have an engagement ring on her finger, but it's not from me!

I guess the moral of the story is to be aware. I trusted him because of the past we shared. I should have also been cautious. I should have not let my feelings get in the way. The only person that will look out for you is you. You need to see things with an open mind, but also knowing that sometimes people aren't as genuine as they claim to be. You have to see the big picture as it is, not how you want it to be. Be away that our minds can rearrange the picture to suit our likings.

# *Chapter 17: Learning Lessons*

I spent many years with Brian. I also suffered much heartache because of him. Those years taught me many things. I do know that I cannot blame Brian for the way things turned out. If it were meant to be, it would have been. But it will not be meant to be because I manipulated the situation so it will turn out as I wish.

If nothing else, I've now learned the few questions that are essential to ask when I meet someone. I could have saved myself lots and lots of time and heartache if I had asked these questions to begin with. I think I always was aware of what he did (the pot smoking) but never followed through by just simply asking for more clarity. Truth is, I didn't want to know.

Brian even told me once that he did, in fact, smoke pot. He wanted 'no secrets' as he put it; so one afternoon we had a long discussion about everything possible. I remember the words 'I smoke pot' very clearly. I did not turn him away though. I thought he 'smoked pot' like my friend, Sherry, smoked pot - once in a blue moon. In fact, the only time I knew that she did it was when she went with Brian to a mutual friend's wedding. I just assumed that was the case with him, too.

If you're just assuming something, as I was, you can't blame the other for the end result. You do have to be strong enough to find out what really is regarding the situation. You also have to be clear enough to let the other know what your views are. You have to be clear on what you will and will not put up with. When you're clear about that, you are letting other know where you draw the line. Then you have to be strong enough if they try to cross that line.

So, the lesson I learned was to simply just always ask. Seeing as I am so against the two things Brian did the most for fun, the first two questions I need to ask are 'do you drink excessively and do you do drugs'? In addition to knowing to ask those two questions, is having the strength to walk away if the answers are not to my liking. When you first meet someone you're on cloud nine, and you don't want to ruin that feeling. It will save heartache in the end though.

You need to realize that you are better than just settling for something you find unacceptable. Instead of wasting your time in a relationship that is not to your liking, find the strength to stand up for yourself and your views. Your views and beliefs are not wrong, they are your views and your beliefs and you have the right to believe in them.

A key element is knowing that there is a slim chance if any that you will be able to change the other person's views and beliefs. Would you even want to be with somebody who is so weak in their beliefs that you can push them around? The change in them will not last for long either. They may change for a brief period of time, but my experience with this sort of situation is that there is little chance someone will change just because you want them to; at least not for very long.

You may feel alone in your views, but know that you are not. There are many others out there that have the same views and beliefs as you. You will learn that once you can hang on to those views and beliefs, others will show up who share what your views and beliefs are. You might have to dig deep to learn how to hold on to them, but the good that will come to you is beyond your wildest dreams.

You are meant to be who you are meant to be and to be in a relationship that you want. Even if it takes going thru bad relationship after bad relationship you will come out stronger in the end. Isn't there a saying that talks about how one bad apple does not spoil the bunch? Eventually you find a good one. Know that they are out there and don't give up on your chance to find one.

I'm not saying Brian was a bad apple. We just lived in very different ways and believed very different things. We just weren't meant to be together. It took me quite awhile to come to that conclusion and to be strong enough to walk away. I think I knew a lot earlier, but I was stubborn so I kept hold of the hope I could help guide him to something better; something better for him and something much better for us as a couple.

You will know that you can deal with the fact that a relationship might not be what you want it to be. Once you stand up for your views, it will feel good to know you are standing up for your convictions and you will know that eventually the right person will come along. It will come faster than you think too.

Nothing good comes from settling for less than you are meant to have. If you do settle for less than you deserve, you can see years that go by before you realize that you are headed towards something you were not meant to have; something you don't want. In the end, the only good that can come out of it is knowing what to do next time you're in this sort of situation.

We can fool ourselves in so many ways. We can talk ourselves into something that we find unacceptable. You have to realize that your life was meant to be so much more than what you're settling for with someone whose views and values are so unmatched to yours. Your life was meant to be great and shared with someone who you don't have to convince yourself that it may be different than your dream life, but you can learn to be happy with this person.

Don't allow yourself to start thinking that this person is probably the best you will ever find. You have to understand that you are very wrong thinking that statement. You will find someone much better suited for you, but you must first let go of the person that is not suited for you.

You must fully let go of what was so that you will be able to receive what can be.

What kept me hanging on for so long was the fear of being alone. I didn't trust in myself to believe that I would be okay. Even though I have taken care of myself all alone in the past, I didn't trust in myself to believe that things would get better. I wanted to avoid the hurt and I was willing to put up with whatever I had to. I didn't and you don't deserve to go through someone treating you badly just to be with that person. You don't have to accept situations or things that you find unacceptable.

I know it may be hard to let go of your dream life, but you must realize that if you have such different views than this person, it is not your dream life you see. You trick yourself into believing this is your dream life, but you are bending your views and beliefs to fit into this person's life. I know it can be scary to be alone, but working on yourself making yourself a better person will help you see your way out of this. It will help you to realize that you are better than putting up with situations you find unacceptable and it will help you to slowly realize that you do deserve better.

I've also learned that I cannot 'save' people. I've learned that we all have our lessons to learn in this life, but they are our lessons. They are not the responsibility of someone else. It is not another's place to show someone the way or impose his or her point of view on someone else. We are all responsible for our own actions and the consequences that come with those actions. We are all free to live our own lives.

It isn't fair to try to force someone else to live the way we believe to be right. In the end, we may just be trying to save the other pain for the consequences that will come from the way they are living. That still doesn't allow us the right to assume the other person will see the wrong of their ways and begin to live our way. The most we can do is be there for the other if choices turn to bad circumstances.

For a while I felt that I had wasted so my years. I don't think they were wasted, though. I don't regret any of the time we spent together. We were on a road and on a path we needed to take to get us to the next step in our lives. I always believed that step was a step we were meant to take together, but I now admit I very much could have been wrong.

I think it was the fear of letting go of what I for so long had hoped for in my life; the happy life of sharing with someone who you loved. For so long I was afraid to be alone, I was afraid of letting go of what I had. Not to mention the thoughts that I could change him; I could make his life better. I thought I alone could change his views and the way he saw and/or thought about things.

I put off what was truly in my heart to do. That is writing. It had always been what I know I'm good at, but I put off focusing on my writing and instead decided to turn my attention towards Brian. I was always so focused on him. In the back of my mind, I knew that was wrong, but I did believe I could make his life better and one day he'd thank me for that.

Looking back I see what a waste of time that was. I see how I put off what was important in my life because I chose to focus on him and his life. And sadly neither one of us is any better off because of that decision. No one will look out for you if you don't look out for yourself. You deserve to live the life of your dreams and you alone can make it happen.

## Chapter 18: Life Goes On

As it is now, Brian and I have totally gone our own separate ways. I do think he's married (still I'm assuming) but I think I'm right. His then fiancé called me one day because I had written him a letter thinking he was out of jail and home. He wasn't home, so she took the letter, read it then threw it away. She obviously got my number in his rolodex. I'm sure by now she's thrown my numbers away so he won't have it. After he got out of jail, I talked to him and told him about the letter. He said he'd never seen it.

Believe it or not, I do hope he's happy. I held on to that dream far too long. During the time we were together I didn't care what was wrong or how we differed. I longed for a husband. That's what you're taught as you grow up; that's the way it's supposed to be. So that is what I set my sights on. I wanted to share my life with someone else. I wanted the white picket fence and 2.5 kids.

And when things are bad you want someone who's there that you can lean on. It's a scary thing to face the world alone. Even if you know you're strong enough, it's not fun to go it alone. As time passes though, you'll realize that as each day does pass you gain more and more strength. You'll soon see that you can do this and one day you'll take a glance over your shoulder and realize that you HAVE been doing this all on your own all along – and you are just fine!

Looking back I wonder how it worked for almost nine years. In my perspective I was the one who made a lot of compromises. I believe that's why it worked for so long, though obviously not perfectly all the time. You always have to make compromises in life, but I think I tried to bend just enough so things would work out within our relationship – even if they weren't always perfect.

All I was doing was postponing the inevitable. I always hoped in the back of my mind that Brian would do an about-face and change his views and change his behavior. I guess there's always a chance and nothing is impossible. But there also comes a time when you have to see how much time you might have wasted and realize that you might have to change your way of thinking and step forward to change that reality.

I wrote this book to let others know they are not alone. I started my website not long after I moved back to Phoenix. There was a time that I couldn't move forward with this book. It was too fresh; the wound was still new and I couldn't even look at it because I still was not over the relationship. Slowly I started my newsletter on my website. It made me feel good knowing I was helping others.

Not all situations are alike but the essence is the same. I know there are a lot of codependent people out there living in situations not of their choosing. Maybe it's not right for you to leave now. Maybe it's not right for you to leave ever; that will be your call. But it is important that you are informed and that you realize that you do have options and what those options are.

Sometimes you can help make things better but sometimes you can't. I guess a lot depends on how much you can put up with. But we shouldn't have to put up with someone who treats us badly or whose life is so very different from ours. You shouldn't have to live the kind of life that you do not find appropriate nor one that is so wrong for you. Sometimes opposites do attract, but sometimes it is also hard to hang on to each other as you maneuver your way through the differences.

I think nothing bad of Brian. In the end, we just weren't meant for each other. He's a good person and I wish him nothing but happiness. I admit it did take a while for me to get to this point. Between trying so hard to bring us back together to beating myself up over not being able to work things out, I spent much more time than I should have on the prospect of 'us'.

What I failed to see is that it wasn't up to just me to fix everything. I tried so hard, but nothing worked. If it was meant to be, Brian would have been there to help fix it. Instead, he was going on with his life, meeting people and in the end getting engaged. I can blame him for leading me on and lying to me about the state our relationship was in and where it was at.

At the same time, it was up to me to be strong enough and smart enough to see things with an open mind and to let go of what was only a dream. After I called him that evening and begged for him to let me come home, he did not automatically say yes and he just drug out the inevitable by asking for a reprieve of 30 days, which then turned into a month after month delay. I was too caught up in my dream life to see it.

I have no hard feeling towards him though. I chose to remember the good we had. The good feeling we once had towards each other and the love we felt for each other. Why should I hang on to the anger I sometimes felt towards him or who's in his life now? The only one that kind of feelings hurt is me. It did take a while, but once I was able to let go of the feelings I had for him, I am thankful for the times we've shared.

If I had it to do over, I think the only thing I would change the way I reacted to a lot of what he did. I'd change my outlook by knowing that I couldn't change him. None of us has the power over another to change their beliefs or their behavior. I know we all think we can, but in the end you'll save yourself a lot of time, frustration and hurt feelings if you realize from the get-go that you can't.

If you're also in this sort of situation, there will always come the time where the only thing you'll feel towards the other person is anger. That's a natural part of the process. I think it's good to go through the process. It will help you to make your way through the anger to the place you need to get to. That way you won't stay stuck and you will get to the other side; the side you need to find your way to.

I do admit there was the time after I found out about Brian's relationship with someone else; I only wished bad things and that things would not work out for him or for them. I wanted him to realize that we were meant for each other; that I was meant to be his and no one else's. I was hurt and angry. He was supposed to be mine and now he was somebody else's. I don't think anyone ever is instantly in the place that you want only good things for an ex.

I think it's important not to hang on to the anger and hurt feelings. Yes, it's likely everyone will go through them, but it is healthy for you to emerge on the other side. To hang on to the anger only brings you more pain and in the end an unhealthy body. It might take a while, but you'll get there.

If it's impossible for you to emerge on the side of wishing your ex the best, it's okay for you to just release the memory. You don't have to have warm fuzzy thoughts for an ex. It will be better for you if you can just liberate yourself enough to let go of any feelings you once had for the other and get yourself to a place that you concentrate on yourself. Focus on the thought that what happened did happen because there's something waiting for you to get to; something so much better.

You now need to build your life to what you want it to be. The relationship might not have worked out as you once envisioned, but it's now time to concentrate on you. Think of what you want to accomplish in your life. Think of your dreams and begin to build them and concentrate on getting yourself to a place where you can realize those dreams. Once you let go of what was you'll see yourself making strides to move toward the life you want.

My hope is to help make your life better (even in some small way). Sometimes just knowing that you are not alone helps. I soon found out there are a lot of people out there living through the same thing. Maybe not the exact same circumstances, but the same hurt feelings, the same stuck feelings of not being able to move your life forward. On the front cover of that Melodie Beattie book I bought not long after returning to Arizona, it said over 4 million copies sold. I thought wow! There are that many people living through this, too?

So, know that you're not alone in your circumstances or your feelings. Stay strong and keep the faith and hopefully you'll arrive at a better destination sooner rather than later. Take one step at a time and move forward no matter how slowly you have to move. Know that you'll get through this. Day by day you'll get stronger. The day will come that you'll look back and you'll see how far you've come and how strong you have become. The day will come you'll see light at the end of the tunnel and know you've made it to the other side of your pain and have arrived at a better life.

Feel free to write to me for anything you might need. My website is: http://loriklauser.com. I wish you peace, strength and happiness always.